Orig. in English

装幀 ● 菊地信義
装画 ● 野村俊夫

解説 ● 岡村昌夫
翻訳 ● 大塚ルシンダ

編集 ●（株）翻訳情報センター

Published by Kodansha International Ltd.,
17-14 Otowa 1-chome, Bunkyo-ku, Tokyo 112.

First Edition 1996

ISBN4-7700-2027-9
97 98 99 10

英語で折り紙
Origami in English

山口 真

はじめに

　折り紙の道に進んで20数年がたちますが、いまだに新鮮な驚きを感じる日々を過ごしています。ほんとうに、いつまでも飽きることのない、奥の深い世界なのです。そして折り紙を続けていて、嬉しく楽しいもうひとつのことは、さまざまな人との出会いです。折り紙を通して知り合った人々が、今では素晴らしい仲間となり、私の最大の財産となっています。

　ここ数年は、海外の友人、知人も増え、年に一度は海外の折り紙協会の集まりにでかけて、新たな折り紙の出会いを楽しんでいます。現在、世界の20数か国に折り紙協会という組織があって、それぞれ独自の活動を続けています。そのおかげで、今やORIGAMIという言葉は国際的になっているのです。

　「折り紙は、だれでも、どこでも、いつでも」――これは1995年に亡くなったアメリカの友人で、素晴らしい折り紙伝道師だったマイケル・シャル氏が信条としていた言葉です。

　この本では、日本人が海外の人に折り方を説明しながら作ることを考えて、対訳にしてみました。海外旅行、留学やホームステイ、あるいは国際交流の場で役に立つことを考えたからです。この本で、あなたと海外の人との素晴らしい出会いのお手伝いができたらいいなと思っています。

山口　真

Preface

It has been more than twenty years since I have been involved in origami, but everyday brings with it a sense of newly-found wonder. I feel that origami is something that one can never lose interest in and the further one delves in it, the more one finds there is to discover. Another great pleasure I have gained from continuing to be involved in origami is meeting many different people. The people I have met through origami are now part of my circle of friends, people who have become very special to me.

During these past years, my circle of friends and acquaintances has grown. I thoroughly enjoy attending the yearly origami convention held overseas to meet more people bound by a common interest in origami. There are now origami associations in twenty different countries throughout the world and each are carrying out their own independent activity which is serving to further disseminate "origami" as a word understood worldwide.

According to an American friend of mine, the late Michael Shall (d. 1995), an enthusiastic origami promoter, origami can be made by anyone, anywhere at anytime.

This book, with explanations written in both Japanese and English, was conceived with the intent of having a Japanese explain to people living overseas how to make origami with both parties attempting them at the same time. I hope this will be of some help in promoting exchanges such as: while traveling, while studying abroad and while staying with a family overseas. I hope this book will aid in promoting memorable encounters with people in other countries.

Yamaguchi Makoto

英 語 で 折 り 紙
Origami in English

目 次　　C O N T E N T S

第1章｜**使える、遊べる折り紙**
Origami That Can Be Used and Played with

日本の折り紙の歴史
◆
The History of Origami
in Japan

作り方の約束記号と
基本の折り方
◆
Symbols and
Basic Folding Techniques

日本の折り紙の歴史

　7世紀の初めに中国から日本に伝えられた紙の製法は、日本ではまもなくその製法や材料が大きく変わり、畳んだり広げたりしても破れない、柔軟で美しい紙が作られるようになりました。この「和紙」と呼ばれる世界に類のない紙が、いろいろな文化を生み出し、その中で「折り紙」が育ってきたのです。

　日本の折り紙がいつごろから作られるようになったのかということは、残念ながらよく分かりません。しかし、手紙を折り畳んだり、紙で物を包むときに折ったりするようなことは古くから行われていたのでしょう。それらが武家社会で発達して様式的に整えられ、実用的また礼法的な折り紙の文化を生み出したのです。しかし、近代になって、特に昭和に入って急速に忘れ去られ、現代では、贈り物に付ける、赤と白の紙を折った飾りである熨斗（のし）などが残っているに過ぎません。

　鶴や舟など、具体的な物の形に見立てて折るものを遊戯折り紙と言います。それらはもともと、病気や不幸などを人間に代わって背負ってくれるように、という意味を持って折られていたものではないかと私は考えています。これらが折られるようになるのは江戸時代に入ったころと思われます。大量生産されるようになった比較的安価な紙が庶民の間に普及していった時代と当然重なります。

　元禄時代ごろ（1700年ごろ）から、折り鶴や数種類の舟などの折り紙が衣装の模様として流行し、さかんに浮世絵などにも描かれるようになりますので、このころから折り紙が急速に広まっていったことが分かります。

The History of Origami in Japan

The technique of paper making, which was introduced into Japan from China during the early seventh century, underwent considerable changes in its manufacturing process in Japan giving rise to a type of paper possessing dual qualities of resilient sturdiness and softness which prevents tearing when it is handled. *Washi*, a unique and distinct type of Japanese paper kindled many forms of cultural creativity, among them origami.

Unfortunately, it is not clear when origami in Japan first originated. However, what is known is that from old, letters and paper to wrap items in were folded. A well-regulated lifestyle came with the advent of samurai society which gave rise to the art of paper folding for practical and formal purposes. Recently, however, particularly from the onset of the Showa period (1926-1989), the art has rapidly passed into oblivion, but a vestige of its former use can still be seen in the *noshi*, a decoration of folded red and white paper attached to a gift.

Origami made to assume concrete shapes of, for example, a crane or boat is regarded as origami for pure enjoyment. However, I feel that these were probably once made for the purpose of bearing the illnesses and misfortunes that befell a person. They began to be made sometime around the beginning of the Edo period (1600-1868) which coincided with an age in which mass-produced, low-priced paper came to be widely used among the people.

During the Genroku era (1688-1704), origami of the crane and several varieties of boats used as designs on clothing became fashionable, and they were also reproduced with great frequency in Ukiyoe prints. Origami rapidly came to have a wide following during this period.

それから約100年後には、折り紙専門の本や刷り物がいろいろ出版されるようになり、多彩で高度な折り紙文化が作られていきました。当時の折り紙は子供の遊びだけでなく、大人の楽しみでもあったため、複雑で折り方の難しいものもたくさんありました。

　一方、ヨーロッパでは、12世紀に製紙法が伝えられて、やがて独自に「折り紙」が生み出されていますが、日本ほど広く厚い折り紙文化の層を持っていた国はありませんでした。

　日本では明治時代には、折り紙は幼稚園や小学校などの教材にもなりました。特に幼稚園では、ドイツの教育家フレーベル（1782―1852）が19世紀の中頃に創始した保育法を大幅に取り入れたのですが、その中にヨーロッパの伝承折り紙と、それから発展させた幾何学的な模様折りなどが含まれていて、以降の日本の折り紙に大きな影響を与えました。

　明治時代だけでも、多くの無名の作者たちの新作がありましたが、一般には、教えられた折り方の通りに折るものとされていたため、大正時代ごろからの創意工夫を重視する教育界の傾向の中で、折り紙は創造的でないという考えが強まったこともあり、社会的に冷遇されていた時期もありました。

　しかし、長い歴史を持つ折り紙文化は見事によみがえり、現代では創作も盛んになり、教育的意味も見直され、豊かな可能性が認識されてきました。大人の趣味としてもかつてない勢いで広まっており、世界各国に愛好家の組織が結成されています。

古典折り紙研究家
岡村　昌夫

About a hundred years later, books and printed matter devoted exclusively to origami were published, creating a diverse and advanced form of origami. They were not only a form of children's amusement, but because they were also intended for adults, many of these origami were difficult to make and incorporated many complicated steps.

The technique of paper making was introduced into Europe in the twelfth century producing a distinct form of origami. However, origami was not taken up by a large number of people as it was in Japan.

During the Meiji period (1868-1912), origami was used as a teaching tool in the kindergarten and elementary school levels. Japan's origami was greatly influenced by Friedrich Wilhelm August Fröbel (1782-1852), a mid-nineteenth century German educator's method of teaching derived from European traditional origami, which further developed into folding to make various geometrical shapes, and was widely adopted particularly in the Japanese kindergartens.

During the Meiji period alone, there were many new origami creations conceived by numerous unknown inventors. However because origami required following precise directions, origami was not well received during the Taisho period (1912-1926), a time when educators favored placing importance on originality and creativity. Origami was deemed as lacking in these qualities. However, braced by a long history, origami once again regained its popularity.

Not only are there now many imaginative and novel origami creations, but its educational worth and immense potential have been also reconsidered and recognized. Origami has gained a widespread following as a hobby among adults. There are now many origami associations that have been formed overseas by origami enthusiasts.

Okamura Masao
Classical Origami Researcher

折り方の約束記号と
基本の折り方
Symbols and Basic
Folding Techniques

折り図を読むためには、折り図記号を理解しなくてはなりません。ここに出てくる記号は、特別むずかしいものではありません。折りはじめる前におぼえて楽しい折り紙を体験してください。

It is necessary to understand the symbols in order to know how to read the diagrams. The symbols that appear here are not too difficult to understand. Know them and enjoy making your own origami!

折り線と記号の種類
Folding lines and Symbols

折り線には谷折り線と山折り線の2種類があります。折る方向を示す記号にも2種類があります。

There are two types of folding lines, the valley fold and the mountain fold. There are also two symbols to indicate the direction of the fold.

- - - - - - - - - - - - - -

谷折り線
Valley Fold

手前で折る
Fold forward

— · — · — · — · — · —

山折り線
Mountain Fold

反対側に折る
Fold to the reverse side

谷折り
Valley Fold

●谷折り線を使って、矢印の方向に折ります。

Fold forward in the direction of the arrow.

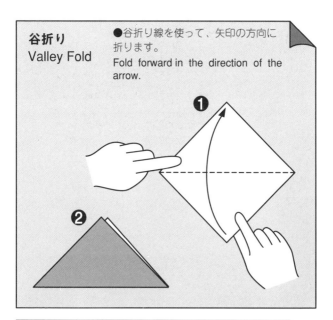

山折り
Mountain Fold

●山折り線を使って、矢印の方向に折ります。

Fold to the reverse side in the direction of the arrow.

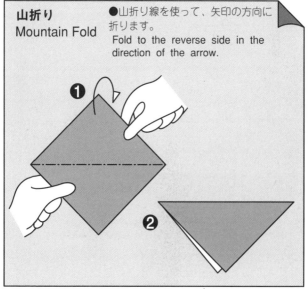

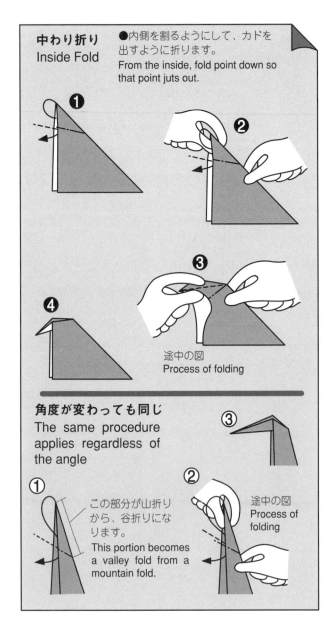

中わり折り
Inside Fold

● 内側を割るようにして、カドを出すように折ります。
From the inside, fold point down so that point juts out.

❶

❷

❸

途中の図
Process of folding

❹

角度が変わっても同じ
The same procedure applies regardless of the angle

③

①
この部分が山折りから、谷折りになります。
This portion becomes a valley fold from a mountain fold.

②
途中の図
Process of folding

かぶせ折り
Cover Fold

●内側を開いて折る部分を裏返すようにしてかぶせるように折ります。

Spread out from the underside and fold over the portion to be folded to form a cover.

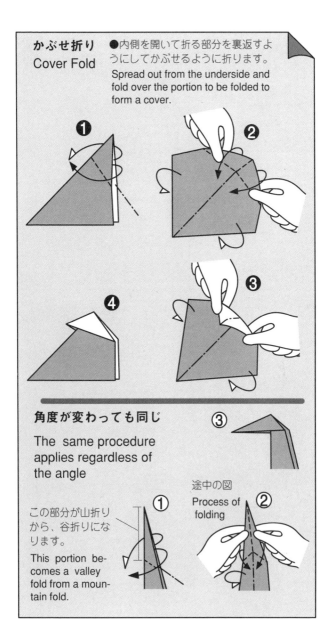

角度が変わっても同じ

The same procedure applies regardless of the angle

この部分が山折りから、谷折りになります。

This portion becomes a valley fold from a mountain fold.

途中の図

Process of folding

次の図が大きくなる
The diagram will be enlarged

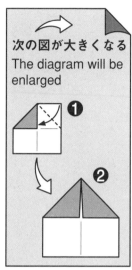

❶

❷

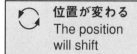

位置が変わる
The position will shift

●次の図が天地の移動など、回転して見る位置が変わるときに使います。
This symbol is used when the figure has undergone a rotation such as from top to bottom.

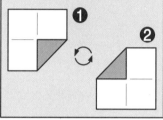

❶

❷

●この記号は、いちど折って折り筋をつけてから戻すという意味です。
This symbol is used to indicate folding to make a crease and returning it to its former position.

折り筋をつける
Make a crease

■実際に折るときには下の図のようにします。
The actual folding is depicted in the lower diagrams.

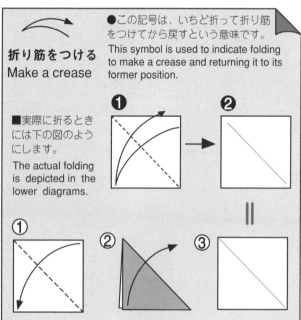

❶

❷

①

②

③

20

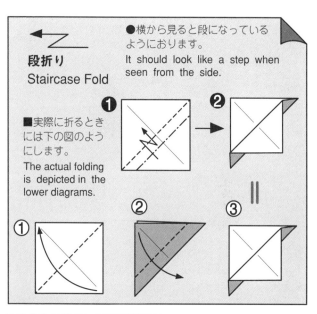

段折り
Staircase Fold

●横から見ると段になっているようにおります。

It should look like a step when seen from the side.

■実際に折るときには下の図のようにします。

The actual folding is depicted in the lower diagrams.

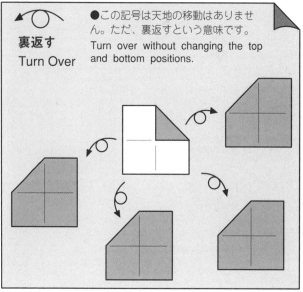

裏返す
Turn Over

●この記号は天地の移動はありません。ただ、裏返すという意味です。

Turn over without changing the top and bottom positions.

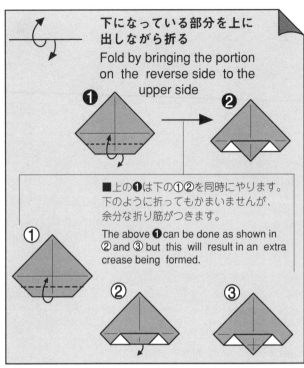

下になっている部分を上に出しながら折る

Fold by bringing the portion on the reverse side to the upper side

■上の❶は下の①②を同時にやります。下のように折ってもかまいませんが、余分な折り筋がつきます。

The above ❶ can be done as shown in ② and ③ but this will result in an extra crease being formed.

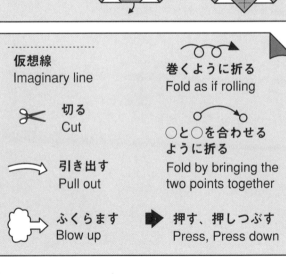

仮想線
Imaginary line

切る
Cut

引き出す
Pull out

ふくらます
Blow up

巻くように折る
Fold as if rolling

○と○を合わせるように折る
Fold by bringing the two points together

押す、押しつぶす
Press, Press down

使える、遊べる折り紙

Origami
That Can Be Used and Played with

かぶと　　Helmet

新聞紙などの大きな紙で折ります。頭にかぶって、昔のサムライの気分を味わってください。

Use a large sheet of paper like a newspaper to make this and enjoy being a samurai!

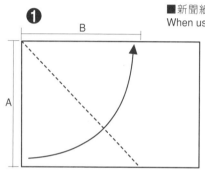

■新聞紙を使った場合
When using a newspaper

①はじめにAの縁を
　Bの縁に合わせる
　ように折ります。
　First align A and B
　edges together and
　fold.

②余分なところを切り
　落として正方形を作
　ります。
　Cut off unneccessary
　portion to form a
　square.

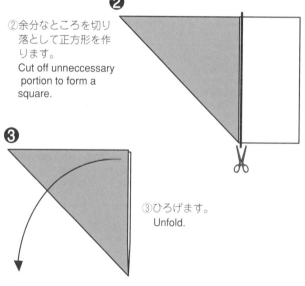

③ひろげます。
　Unfold.

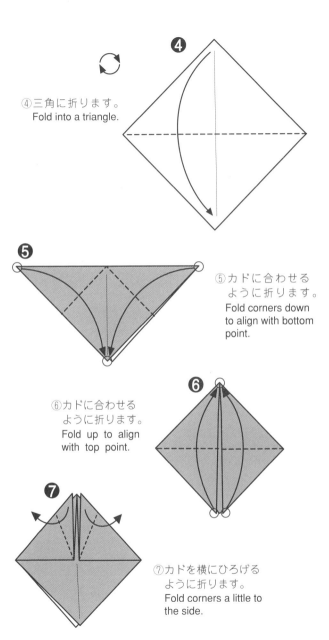

④三角に折ります。
Fold into a triangle.

⑤カドに合わせる
　ように折ります。
Fold corners down
to align with bottom
point.

⑥カドに合わせる
　ように折ります。
Fold up to align
with top point.

⑦カドを横にひろげる
　ように折ります。
Fold corners a little to
the side.

⑧上の1枚だけ折り
　上げます。
Fold only one sheet
up along the line.

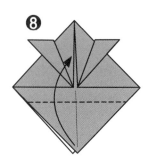

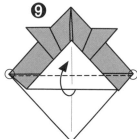

⑨カド(○印)を結ぶ線で
　折り上げます。
Fold up along the line
at (○).

⑩カド(○)を結ぶ線で
　カドを内側に折り込
　みます。
Tuck point inside along
the line at (○).

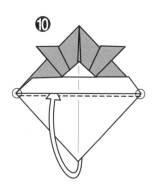

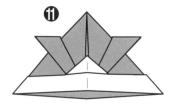

できあがり
Completed
helmet

ひこうき **Airplane**

この飛行機はゆっくりと長く飛びます。だれが長く飛ばすことができるか、競争しましょう。

A leisurely flying plane that can cover a great distance. See whose can fly the longest.

❶

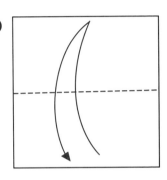

①はじめに横に半分に折って折り筋をつけます。

First fold in half to make a crease.

❷

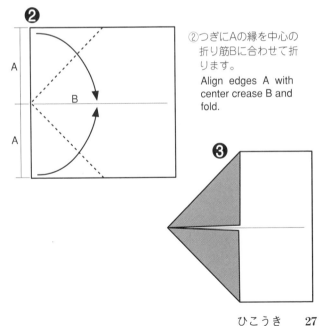

②つぎにAの縁を中心の折り筋Bに合わせて折ります。

Align edges A with center crease B and fold.

❸

裏返します。
Turn over.

④カドを中心に折ります。
　（下にあるカドに合わせ
　ます）
Fold point at middle
to align with corners
on the reverse side.

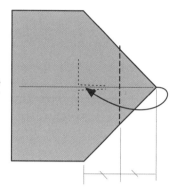

❺

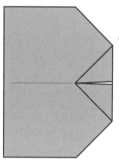

⑤裏返します。
Turn over.

❻

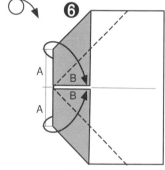

A
B
B
A

⑥Aの縁をBの縁に
　合わせるように
　折ります。
Align edges A with
edges B and fold.

❼

⑦半分に後ろに
　折り上げます。
Fold in half to
the reverse side.

28

⑧Aの縁をBの縁に
合わせるように
折ります。

Align edge A with
edge B and fold.
Do the same on
the reverse side.

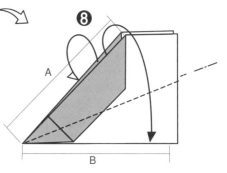

⑨内側からカドを
引き出します。
Pull out point
from the inside.

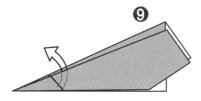

⑩しっかりと折り筋を
つけてから翼を水平
にします。
Fold creases firmly
before bringing up
wings horizontally.

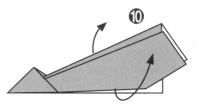

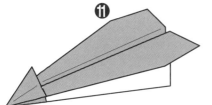

できあがり
Completed
airplane

ひこうき　29

ふうせん **Balloon**

折り紙の代表的な人気の作品です。ふくらませて、ポンポンと掌ではね上げて遊びます。

A popular origami piece. Inflate it and bounce it on the palm of your hand.

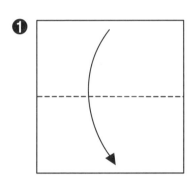

❶

①まず半分に折ります。
First fold in half.

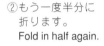 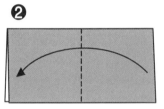

②もう一度半分に折ります。
Fold in half again.

❷

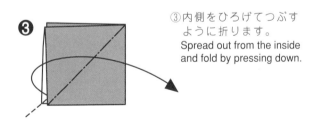

❸

③内側をひろげてつぶすように折ります。
Spread out from the inside and fold by pressing down.

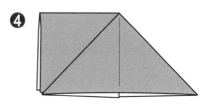

❹裏返します。
Turn over.

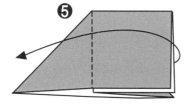

⑤反対側に折り直します。

Swing the edges to the opposite side.

⑥内側をひろげてつぶすように折ります。

Spread out from the inside and fold by pressing down.

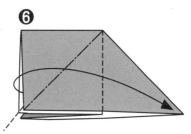

⑦カドに合わせるように折ります。
反対側も同じに折ります。

Bring bottom corners to the top point and fold. Do the same on the reverse side.

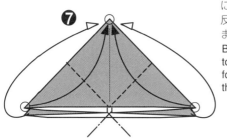

ふうせん　31

⑧カドを中心に合わせる
　ように折ります。
　反対側も同じに折りま
　す。
Bring side corners
to the center and
fold. Do the same
on the reverse side.

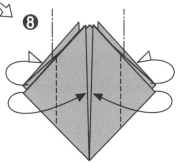

⑨カドを折り下げます。
Fold corners down.

⑩縁のところで折って
　折り筋をつけます。
Fold along the dotted
line to make a crease.

⑪カドをすき間に
　折り込みます。
Tuck corners
into the pockets.

⑫反対側も同じに折り
ます。
Do the same on the
reverse side.

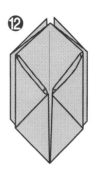

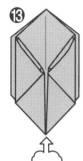

⑬ふくらまし
ます。
Blow into the
opening.

できあがり
Completed
balloon

[遊び方]
水を入れて飛ばして遊んでも
おもしろいです。

For more fun
Add water and throw.

グローブ **Glove**

新聞紙などを使って折ります。
本当にキャッチボールができる
ので、折って遊んでください。

Use a newspaper to make
this. You can really play
catch with it. Enjoy!

①新聞紙のような長方形の
　紙を使い、はじめに縦、
　横半分に折り筋をつけま
　す。

Use a rectangular sheet
of paper like a newspaper.
Make a crease along the
length and width.

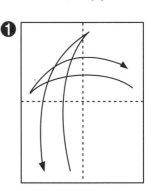

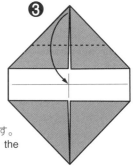

②Aの縁をBの折り筋に合わ
　せるように折ります。

Align edges A with crease
B and fold.

③カドを中心に折ります。
Fold point down to the
center.

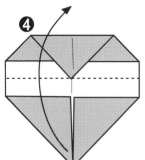

❹ ④中心の折り筋のところから
　　折り上げます。
　Fold up along the center
　crease line.

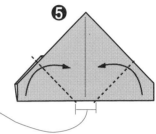

❺

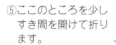

⑤ここのところを少し
　すき間を開けて折り
　ます。
　Fold leaving a little
　space here.

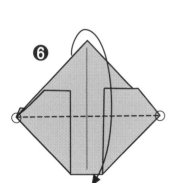

❻

⑥カド(○印)を結ぶ線で
　折り下げます。
　Fold point down along
　the line at (○).

❼

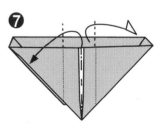

⑦内側をひろげて立体に
　します。
　Spread the inside open
　to give it fullness and
　bring the opposite
　corners together.

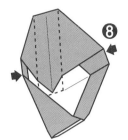

⑧

⑧途中の図
What it should look like
when it is being spread
open.

⑨

⑨手のはいるところを
ひろげます。
Widen the aperture
for the hand to go
through.

⑩

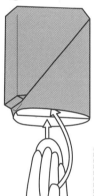

できあがり
Completed
glove

⑩すき間に手を
入れて使いま
す。
Slip fingers in
through the
aperture.

[遊び方] 紙を丸めたボールを
作って遊んでください。
本物のボールでもとれ
ます。

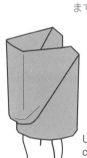

For more fun

Use a ball made from
crumpled paper. It even
works with a real ball.

ぴょんぴょん かえる Jumping Frog

このカエルは折り紙のくせ
にピョンと跳びます。子ど
もたちに人気の作品です。

This frog really jumps! An
origami popular with children.

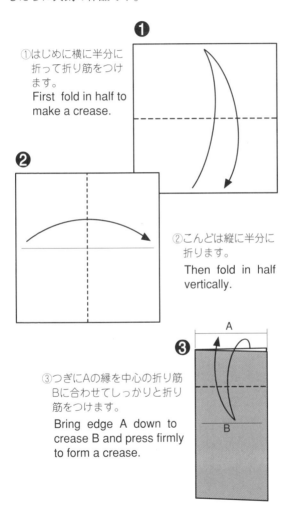

❶

①はじめに横に半分に
折って折り筋をつけ
ます。
First fold in half to
make a crease.

❷

②こんどは縦に半分に
折ります。
Then fold in half
vertically.

❸

③つぎにAの縁を中心の折り筋
Bに合わせてしっかりと折り
筋をつけます。
Bring edge A down to
crease B and press firmly
to form a crease.

❹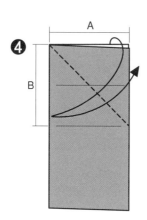

④Aの縁をBの縁に合わせる
　ようにしてしっかりと折
　り筋をつけます。

Align edge A with edge B and
press firmly to form a crease.

❺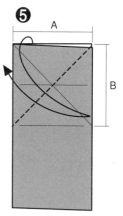

⑤Aの縁をBの縁に合わせる
　ようにしてしっかりと折
　り筋をつけます。

Align edge A with edge B and
press firmly to form a crease.

❻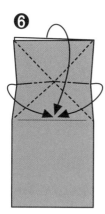

⑥❸～❺でつけた折り筋
　通りに折りたたみます。

Push in sides and fold
along the creases made
in ❸ to ❺ .

 ❼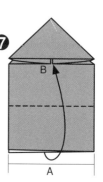

⑦Aの縁をBの縁に合わ
　せるように折ります。

Bring edge A up to
edge B and fold.

⑧Aの縁を中心に合わ
せるように折ります。
上の方は三角部分の
下になります。

Bring sides A to the
center and fold. The
upper part of the fold
should go under the
triangle.

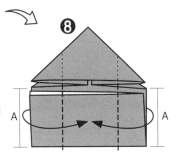

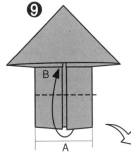

⑨Aの縁をBの縁に合わ
せるように折ります。

Bring edge A up to edge
B and fold.

⑩Aの縁をBの縁に合わせる
ようにして折ります。

Align edges A with edge
B and fold.

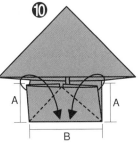

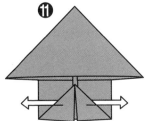

⑪カドを引き出して
つまむように折り
ます。

Draw out the inside
corners.

ぴょんぴょんかえる　　**39**

⑫カドを下に折り
直します。
Lower corners.

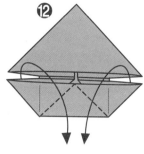

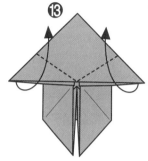

⑬カドを斜めに折り
上げます。
Fold corners up
diagonally.

⑭横にひろげるように
折ります。
Fold bottom corners
diagonally .

このカドに合わ
せるとよいです。
Fold to this corner
(○).

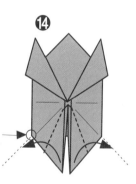

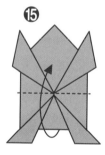

⑮中心のところから
折り上げます。
Fold at middle.

⑯

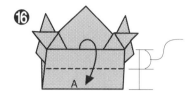

こちらの幅を少し
細くします。
Make width a little
narrower here.

⑯下の縁 A より少し手前に折ります。
Fold down so that it does not touch
edge A.

⑰ここのところが
少し開くように
折ります。
Leave this part
open a little.

⑰

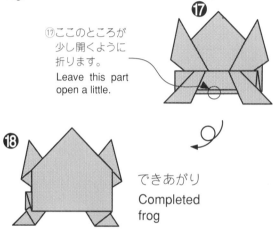

⑱

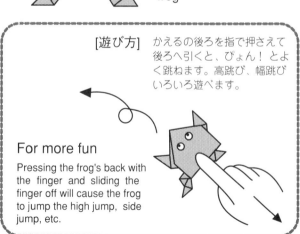

できあがり
Completed
frog

[遊び方]　かえるの後ろを指で押さえて
後ろへ引くと、ぴょん！とよ
く跳ねます。高跳び、幅跳び
いろいろ遊べます。

For more fun

Pressing the frog's back with
the finger and sliding the
finger off will cause the frog
to jump the high jump, side
jump, etc.

はばたく はと Flapping **Pigeon**

羽がはばたく、楽しい動く折り紙の作品です。とくに子どもたちに人気のある折り紙です。

A delightful pigeon that flutters its wings. Popular with children.

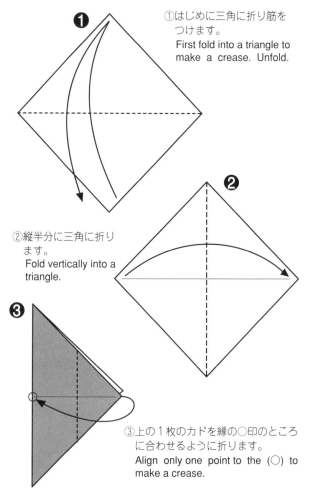

❶

①はじめに三角に折り筋をつけます。
First fold into a triangle to make a crease. Unfold.

❷

②縦半分に三角に折ります。
Fold vertically into a triangle.

❸

③上の１枚のカドを縁の○印のところに合わせるように折ります。
Align only one point to the (○) to make a crease.

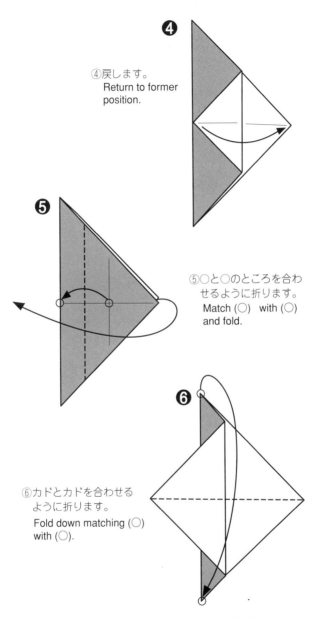

④戻します。
Return to former
position.

⑤○と○のところを合わ
せるように折ります。
Match (○) with (○)
and fold.

⑥カドとカドを合わせる
ように折ります。
Fold down matching (○)
with (○).

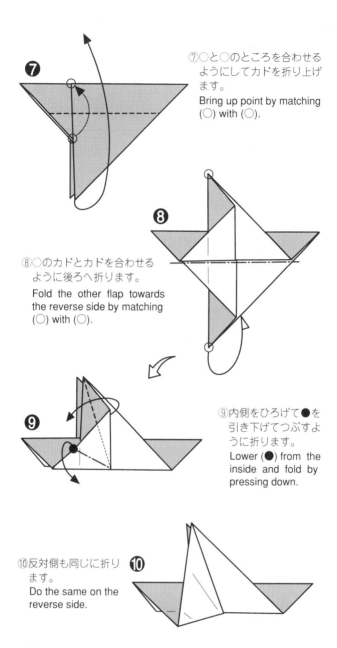

⑦○と○のところを合わせる
ようにしてカドを折り上げ
ます。
Bring up point by matching
(○) with (○).

⑧○のカドとカドを合わせる
ように後ろへ折ります。
Fold the other flap towards
the reverse side by matching
(○) with (○).

⑨内側をひろげて●を
引き下げてつぶすよ
うに折ります。
Lower (●) from the
inside and fold by
pressing down.

⑩反対側も同じに折り
ます。
Do the same on the
reverse side.

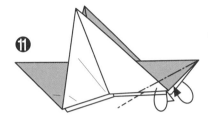

⑪それぞれカドを
内側に折ります。
Fold tips to the
inside.

⑫カドを中わり折りで
出してくちばしを作
ります。
Fold point down from
the inside to form a
beak.

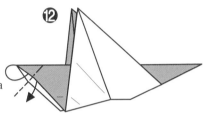

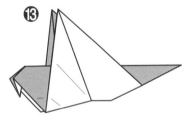

できあがり
Completed
pigeon

[遊び方] 図のように持って左右に
引いたりゆるめたりすると
パタパタとよくはばたきます。

For more fun

Hold as shown in the diagram.
Pull and release to make wings
flap.

おしゃべり からす　Talking **Crow**

くちばしを、ぱくぱくさせ
ておしゃべりします。くち
ばしで、物をくわえること
もできます。

A crow that can talk by opening and closing its beak. It
can also hold something in it.

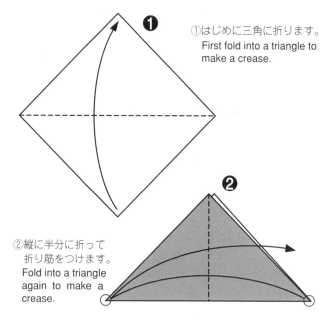

①はじめに三角に折ります。
First fold into a triangle to
make a crease.

②縦に半分に折って
折り筋をつけます。
Fold into a triangle
again to make a
crease.

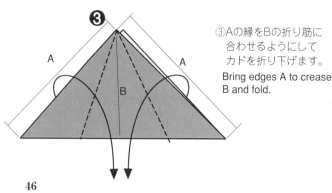

③Aの縁をBの折り筋に
合わせるようにして
カドを折り下げます。
Bring edges A to crease
B and fold.

46

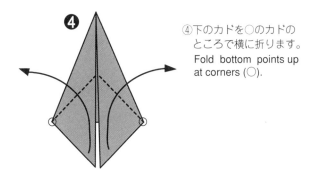

❹

④下のカドを○のカドの
　ところで横に折ります。
Fold bottom points up
at corners (○).

❺

⑤内側のカドを引き離すように
　してはがします。
Separate the two overlapping
points.

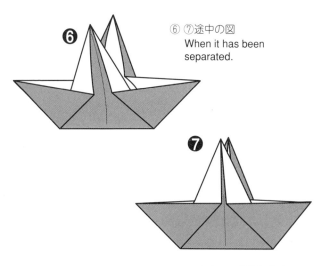

❻

⑥ ⑦途中の図
　When it has been
　separated.

❼

裏返します。
Turn over.

⑧上の1枚のカドを縁の
○印のところに合わせ
るように折ります。
On the reverse side, fold
one point down to (○).

❽

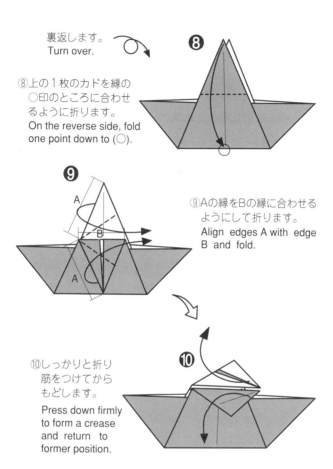

❾

⑨Aの縁をBの縁に合わせる
ようにして折ります。
Align edges A with edge
B and fold.

⑩しっかりと折り
筋をつけてから
もどします。
Press down firmly
to form a crease
and return to
former position.

❿

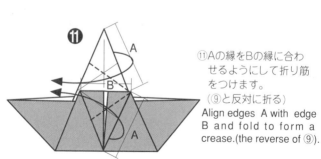

⓫

⑪Aの縁をBの縁に合わ
せるようにして折り筋
をつけます。
（⑨と反対に折る）
Align edges A with edge
B and fold to form a
crease.(the reverse of ⑨).

⑫縦に半分に後ろに
　折ります。
Fold in half vertically
to the reverse side.

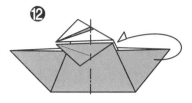

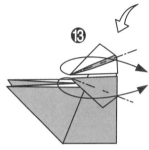

⑬くちばしになるカドを
　つまむように折ります。

Fold along the dotted
lines to form a crease.
Unfold. Pull points out to
the right to form a beak.

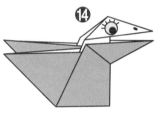

できあがり
Completed
crow

[遊び方]　羽を持って左右に動かすと
　　　　　くちばしをパクパクさせて
　　　　　おしゃべりします。

For more fun

Moving the wings back and forth
will cause the bird to open and
close its beak.

紙コップ Paper Cup

身近な紙がコップに変身する楽しい折り紙です。紙を2枚使うともっと丈夫になります。

A fun-to-make origami that can transform an ordinary sheet of paper into a cup. Use two sheets for sturdiness.

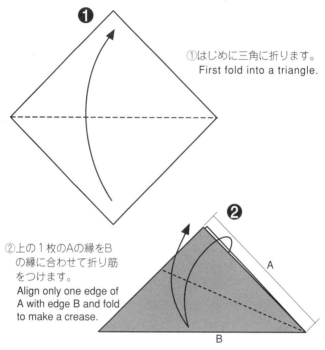

①はじめに三角に折ります。
First fold into a triangle.

②上の1枚のAの縁をBの縁に合わせて折り筋をつけます。
Align only one edge of A with edge B and fold to make a crease.

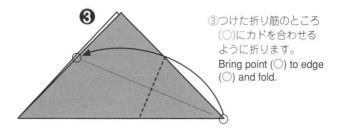

③つけた折り筋のところ（○）にカドを合わせるように折ります。
Bring point (○) to edge (○) and fold.

④カドとカドを合わせる
　ように折ります。
　Bring (○) together and
　fold.

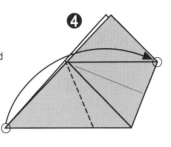

⑤折った部分にかぶせるよう
　に上の1枚だけ折り下げま
　す。

Bring only one point down
to cover the folded portion.

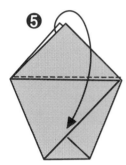

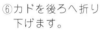

⑥カドを後ろへ折り
　下げます。
　Fold the other point
　down on the reverse
　side.

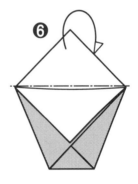

できあがり
Completed
paper cup

コースター Coaster

実用性の高い作品です。パーティーなどで，皆の目の前で作ってあげるのはいかが？

An origami that can be put to practical use. Why not make a personal one on the spot for everyone at a party?

折り紙2枚 Two origami sheets

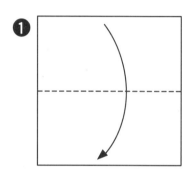

❶

15～17センチぐらいの正方形の紙で折ると使えます。

This coaster can be utilized by using a 15-17 cm (6-7 inch) sq. piece of paper.

①はじめに半分に折ります。

First fold in half.

②半分に折ったらもういちど半分に折って折り筋をつけます。

Fold in half again to make a crease.

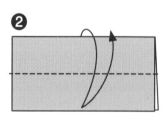

❷

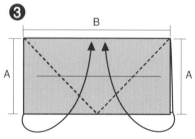

❸

B

A   A

③Aの縁をBに合わせて三角に折ります。

Align edges A with edge B and fold into a triangle.

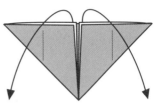

④しっかりと折り筋をつけてから
　戻します。
Press firmly to make a crease
and return to former position.

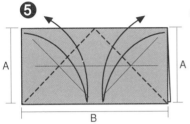

⑤反対側も同じようにして、
　A の縁をB に合わせて三角
　に折ってしっかりと折り筋
　をつけます。
Do the same on the oppo-
site side. Align edges A with
edge B, press firmly to form
a crease and return to former
position.

⑥上の一枚だけ
　広げます。
Unfold.

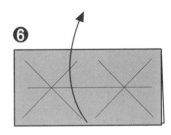

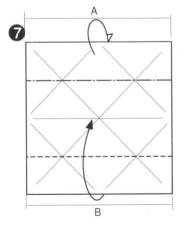

⑦❷でつけた折り筋を使って
　A の縁を後ろへ、Bの縁を
　手前に、それぞれ中心の折
　り筋に合わせるように折り
　ます。
Fold edge A to the reverse
side along the crease line
and fold edge B forward
along the crease line.

❽

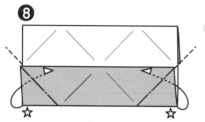

⑧それぞれ☆のカドを
内側に折り込みます。

Tuck corners (☆) in
from the inside along
the crease line and
fold.

❾

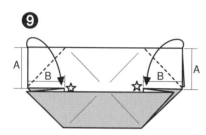

⑨A の縁をB の縁に
合わせて三角に折
ります。

Align edges A with
edges B and fold
into a triangle.

❿

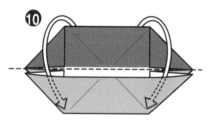

⑩上の▰▰の部分を
❽❾で折ったカド
にかぶせるように
すき間に折り込み
ます。

Tuck the shaded
part into the fold
formed in ❽ and ❾.

⓫

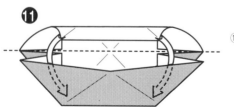

⑪途中の図
Tucking into
the fold.

54

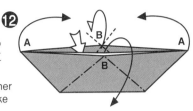

⑫Aのカドを上げながら
　Bの所を広げるように
　して平らにします。
Bring corners A together
and widen B to make
level.

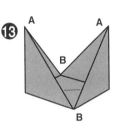

⑬

できあがり
Completed
coaster

おしゃれな紙を選んで作ると、
パーティーなどでも充分使える
ものができ、大活躍します。
Using fancy paper will transform
this coaster into something elegant, even for use at a party.

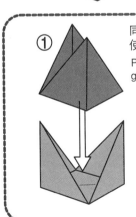

①

②

同じものを2つ作って組んで
使ってもおもしろいです。
Pair two similar ones for a varie-
gated effect.

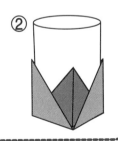

ナプキンリング Napkin Ring

親しい方々を招いたときな
どのパーティーなどで使う
と、とても喜ばれ重宝され
ます。

Make individual ones for everyone when inviting close friends
to a party. The personal touch
will surely be appreciated.

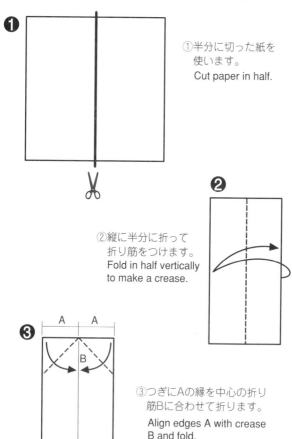

❶

①半分に切った紙を
使います。
Cut paper in half.

❷

②縦に半分に折って
折り筋をつけます。
Fold in half vertically
to make a crease.

❸
A   A
B

③つぎにAの縁を中心の折り
筋Bに合わせて折ります。

Align edges A with crease
B and fold.

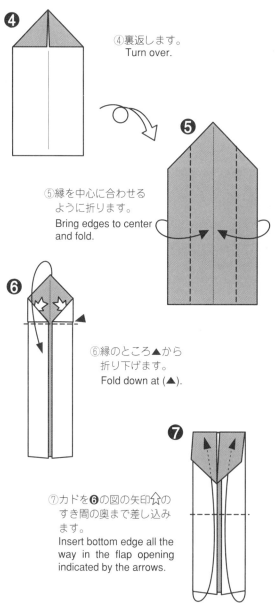

❹ ④裏返します。
Turn over.

⑤縁を中心に合わせる
ように折ります。
Bring edges to center
and fold.

❺

❻ ⑥縁のところ▲から
折り下げます。
Fold down at (▲).

❼ ⑦カドを❻の図の矢印⇧の
すき間の奥まで差し込み
ます。
Insert bottom edge all the
way in the flap opening
indicated by the arrows.

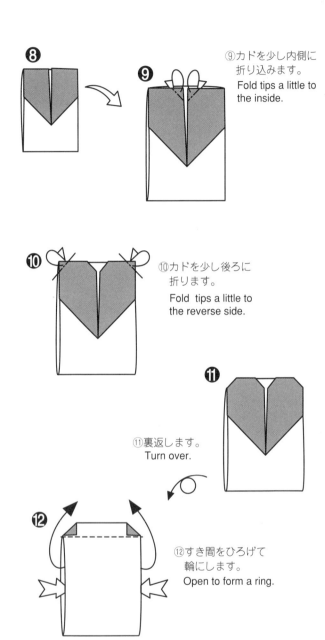

⑧

⑨

⑨カドを少し内側に
折り込みます。
Fold tips a little to
the inside.

⑩

⑩カドを少し後ろに
折ります。
Fold tips a little to
the reverse side.

⑪

⑪裏返します。
Turn over.

⑫

⑫すき間をひろげて
輪にします。
Open to form a ring.

58

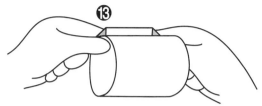

⑬ ⑩で折ったカドをかぶせる
ようにしっかりと折ります。
Press corners made in ⑩
firmly down onto ring.

⑭裏返します。
Turn over.

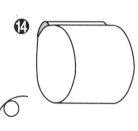

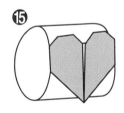

できあがり
Completed
napkin ring

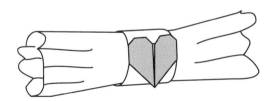

鳥の入れ物 Bird Receptacle

キャンディーなどを入れて
テーブルの上に置くと楽し
いものです。贈り物入れに
も最適。

A delightful piece when filled
with candies and placed on a
table. Great as a receptacle
to place a gift in.

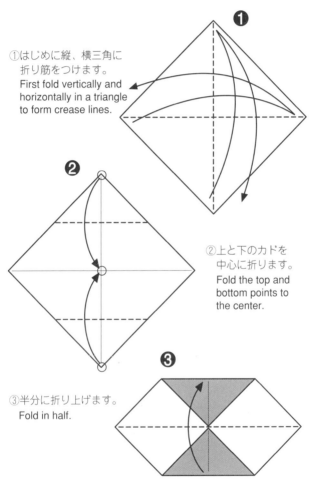

①はじめに縦、横三角に
　折り筋をつけます。
First fold vertically and
horizontally in a triangle
to form crease lines.

②上と下のカドを
　中心に折ります。
Fold the top and
bottom points to
the center.

③半分に折り上げます。
Fold in half.

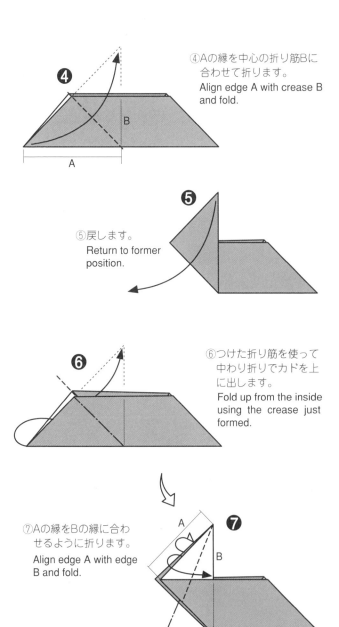

④Aの縁を中心の折り筋Bに
　合わせて折ります。
　Align edge A with crease B
　and fold.

⑤戻します。
　Return to former
　position.

⑥つけた折り筋を使って
　中わり折りでカドを上
　に出します。
　Fold up from the inside
　using the crease just
　formed.

⑦Aの縁をBの縁に合わ
　せるように折ります。
　Align edge A with edge
　B and fold.

⑧カドを真上に折り上げて
しっかりと折り筋をつけ
ます。

Fold point up and press
firmly to make a crease.
Return to former position.

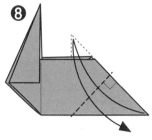

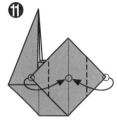

⑨つけた折り筋を使って
中わり折りでカドを上
に出します。

Fold up from the inside
using the crease line as
a guide.

⑩右のカドを反対側に
折ります。

Swing one point to
the opposite side.

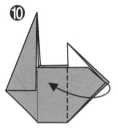

⑪左右のカドを中心に
折ります。

Bring left and right
points to the center
and fold.

⑫閉じます。
Close.

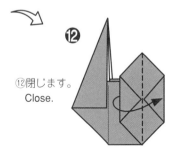

⑬カドを中わり折りで
　出します。
Bring point down from
the inside.

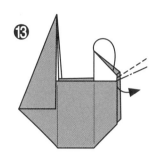

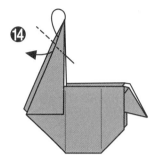

⑭カドを中わり折りで出して
　くちばしを作ります。
Bring point down to form a
beak.

⑮カド(○印)を結ぶ線で
　折り筋をつけます。
Fold corners at (○) to
make a crease.

⑯内側をひろげて■の
　部分を平らにします。
Spread the inside open
and flatten the shaded
portion.

できあがり
Completed
bird receptacle

鳥の入れ物　63

ギフトボックス **Gift Box**

しっかりした紙で折ると、どんなものを入れても大丈夫です。好きな色の紙を使いましょう。

Almost anything can be placed in this box if made with sturdy paper. Make it in your favorite color.

折り紙2枚 Two origami sheets

[本体] Box

①はじめに半分に折り筋をつけます。

First fold in half to form a crease.

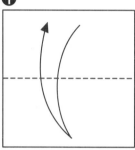

②★のカドのところから○のカドをつけた折り筋の上に合わせるように折ります。

Bring (○) corner to (○) crease and fold using (★) as a pivot.

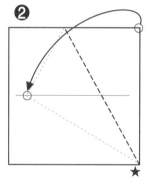

③しっかりと折り筋をつけてから戻します。

Press down firmly to form a crease and return to former position.

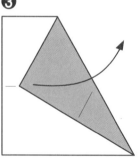

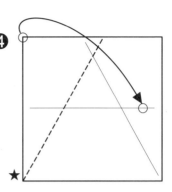

④★のカドのところから
　○のカドをつけた折り
　筋の上に合わせるよう
　に折ります。

Bring (○) corner to (○)
crease and fold using
(★) as a pivot.

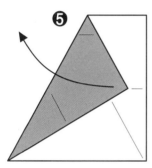

⑤しっかりと折り筋をつけて
　から戻します。

Press down firmly to form a
crease and return to former
position.

⑥つけた折り筋が重なった
　ところ○で折ります。

Fold edge down at where
the creases intersect at (○).

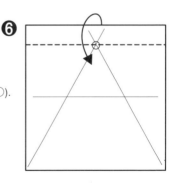

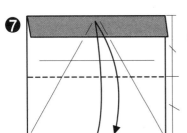

❼⑦半分に折り筋をつけます。
Fold in half to form a crease.

⑧★のカドのところから○のカドをつけた折り筋の上に合わせるように折ります。
Bring (○) corner to (○) crease and fold using (★) as a pivot.

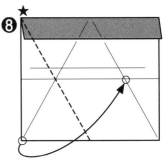

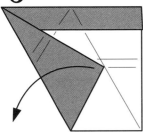

⑨しっかりと折り筋をつけてから戻します。
Press down firmly to form a crease and return to former position.

⑩★のカドのところから○のカドをつけた折り筋の上に合わせるように折ります。
Bring (○) corner to (○) crease and fold using (★) as a pivot.

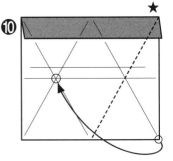

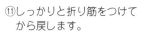

⑪しっかりと折り筋をつけて
から戻します。

Fold down firmly to form a
crease and return to former
position.

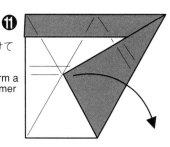

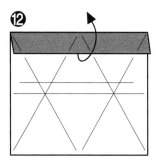

⑫戻します。

Return to former
position.

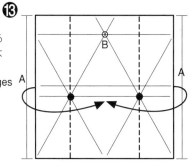

⑬Aの縁を●のところから
中心Bの○に合わせるよ
うに折ります。

Fold at (●) to bring edges
A to center B.

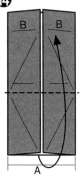

⑭Aの縁をBの折り筋
に合わせるように折
ります。

Bring up edge A to
crease B.

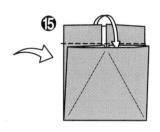

⑮ついている折り筋を使って
内側に折り込みます。

Using the crease already
formed, insert edge into the
pocket.

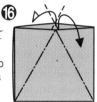

⑯❷から⓫でつけた折り筋を使って
内側をひろげて立体にします。

Using the creases made in ❷ to
⓫, open the inside to form a
cubic figure.

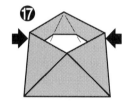

⑰途中の図

How it should
look like.

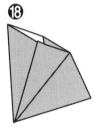

[本体]の
できあがり

Completion
of the box

[紙の比率]

Comparison of size of
paper used to make
the stopper.

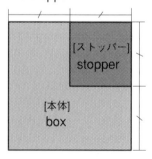

[ストッパー]は[本体]の1/4か
それよりやや小さめの紙を使
います。

The size of the paper used to
make the stopper should be
1/4 or less of the one used to
make the box.

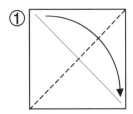

① はじめに三角に折り筋を
つけてから三角に折りま
す。

First fold into a triangle.

[ストッパー]
Stopper

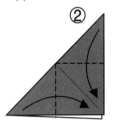

② カドとカドを合わせる
ように折ります。

Bring corners to point
and fold.

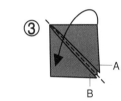

③ 半分に折ります。
Fold in half.

④ 下になっているストッパーの
AとBのカドを向こう側と手
前のすき間に差し込みます。

Pinch opening of cubic box
shut and insert A and B flaps
of stopper into the folds of the
box to form a covering over
the opening.

できあがり
Completed
gift box

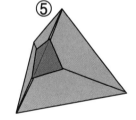

用　紙　を　選　ぶ
Choosing the Right Paper

作品によって素材を使い分けることで、折り紙はさらに興味深いものとなります。

第1章の実用折り紙や、第3章の飾りや小物などは、紙を選びます。例えば、厚手で、しっかりした紙がよいとか、プリント柄付きの紙を使うなど工夫することで、幅がぐっと広がり、実用に耐えるものができます。特にクリスマス作品は、用紙や色によって違いがはっきり出ます。

手軽に使える素材の一つとして、包装紙をカットして使用してみることをお奨めします。今までとは違った折り紙の雰囲気が味わえることでしょう。

ときには全く違った発想で素材を変えてみるのも面白いでしょう。布を用いて、アイロンで折るなど、まだまだいろいろ考えることができます。

Selecting the right paper according to use will greatly enhance the appearance of the origami creation.

Different types of paper such as stiff hard paper and printed paper are used in Chapter 1 "Origami That Can Be Used and Played with," and Chapter 3 "Charming Decorative Accessories." The right paper will broaden the range of utilization of the origami piece, as well as making it able to withstand wear. Different colors and types of paper are used especially in the Christmas pieces giving it a unique flavor.

A material readily available is wrapping paper. Wrapping paper cut in an appropriate size and folded can transform the appearance of any piece.

Using an entirely different material altogether may bring surprising results. For example, cloth can be folded into origami by ironing. There are many other materials available that can be used to create origami.

第 2 章
Chapter Two

かわいい動物、植物
Delightful Animals and Plants

つ　る　　Crane

つるは日本では平和のシン
ボルの鳥として親しまれて
きました。折り紙の代名詞
的な作品です。

In Japan, the crane is a symbol of peace. the origami of
the crane has become syn-
onymous with origami itself.

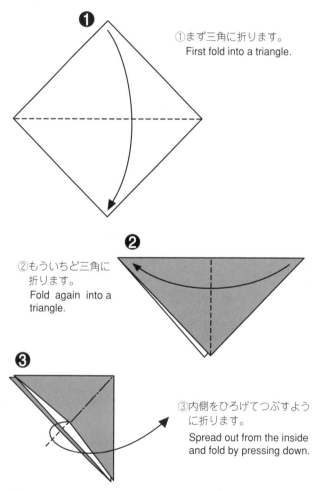

❶

①まず三角に折ります。
First fold into a triangle.

❷

②もういちど三角に
折ります。
Fold again into a
triangle.

❸

③内側をひろげてつぶすよう
に折ります。

Spread out from the inside
and fold by pressing down.

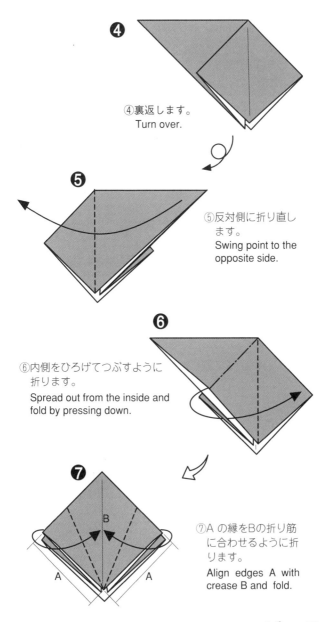

❹ ④裏返します。
Turn over.

❺ ⑤反対側に折り直し
ます。
Swing point to the
opposite side.

❻ ⑥内側をひろげてつぶすように
折ります。
Spread out from the inside and
fold by pressing down.

❼ B
A A
⑦A の縁をBの折り筋
に合わせるように折
ります。
Align edges A with
crease B and fold.

つる　73

❽

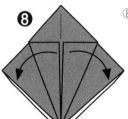

⑧しっかりと折り筋をつけ
てから戻します。

Press down firmly on the
fold before returning to
its former position.

❾

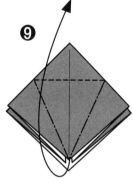

⑨つけた折り筋を使って内側
をひろげてつぶすように折
ります。

Spread out from the inside
and fold by pressing down
using the creases just made.

❿

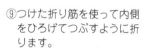

⑩反対側も同じに折り
ます。
Do the same on the
reverse side.

⓫

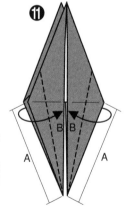

⑪A の縁をBの縁に合
わせるように折りま
す。
Align edges A with
center crease B and
fold.

74

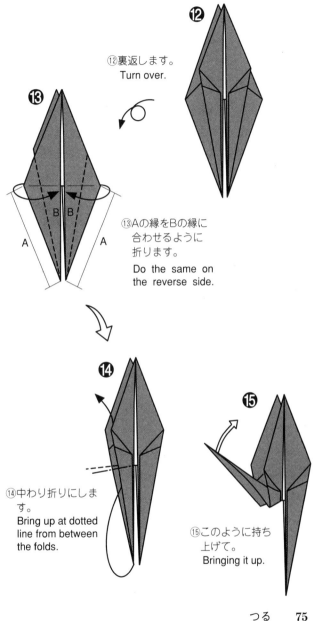

⑫裏返します。
Turn over.

⑫

⑬

⑬Aの縁をBの縁に
合わせるように
折ります。

Do the same on
the reverse side.

A　B　B　A

⑭

⑭中わり折りにしま
す。
Bring up at dotted
line from between
the folds.

⑮

⑮このように持ち
上げて。
Bringing it up.

つる　75

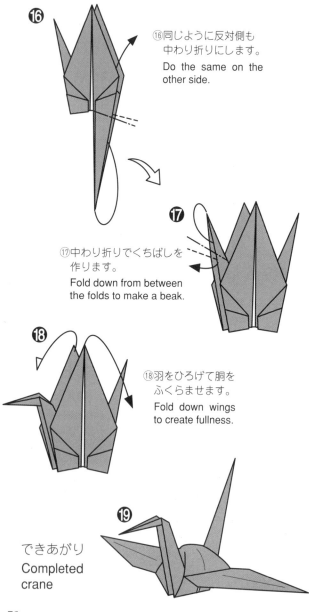

⑯

⑯同じように反対側も
中わり折りにします。

Do the same on the
other side.

⑰

⑰中わり折りでくちばしを
作ります。

Fold down from between
the folds to make a beak.

⑱

⑱羽をひろげて胴を
ふくらませます。

Fold down wings
to create fullness.

⑲

できあがり
Completed
crane

白　鳥　Swan

黒い紙で折れば黒鳥にもな
ります。ナプキンペーパー
で折ってテーブルに飾って
もいいですね。

Use black paper to make an
elegant black swan, and
decorative paper to make a
delightful centerpiece.

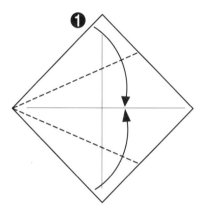

①初めに縦横半分に折り
　筋をつけてから縁を中
　心に合わせるように折
　ります。

First fold into a triangle
to make a crease.
Unfold. Then fold edges
to the crease as shown
in the diagram.

②つぎにAの縁を中心の
　折り筋Bに合わせて折
　ります。

Align edges A with cen-
ter crease B and fold.

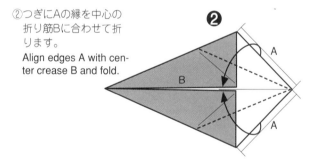

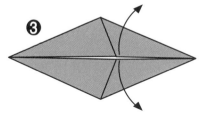

③しっかりと折り筋を
　つけてから戻します。

Press down firmly
and return to former
position.

④つけた折り筋を利用してカド
　を内側に折り込みます。

Using the creases just made,
transpose the upper and lower
flaps. The upper flap should
now be at the bottom.

❹

❺

⑤裏返します。
Turn over.

⑥内側のカドギリギリの○の
　ついたところから折ります。
Fold at (○) at the very limit.

❻

❼

⑦縁のところから三角に
　折ります。

Fold points along the
edge to form a triangle.

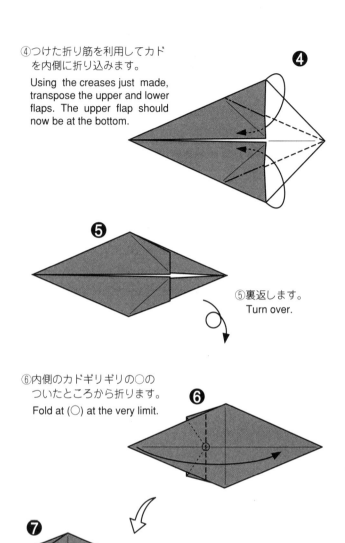

78

⑧図のように中心の線
（▼）に合わせて折り
返します。

Fold point back at
center line (▼) as
shown in the diagram.

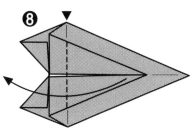

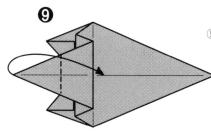

⑨カドが少しはみ出るよ
うにさらに折り返しま
す。

Fold point back again
so that it juts out a little
beyond the center line.

⑩半分に折ります。
Fold in half.

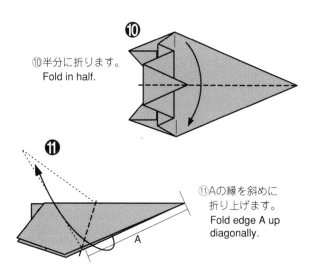

⑪Aの縁を斜めに
折り上げます。
Fold edge A up
diagonally.

白鳥　79

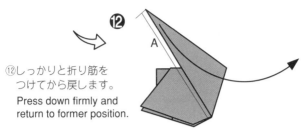

⑫しっかりと折り筋を
　つけてから戻します。

Press down firmly and
return to former position.

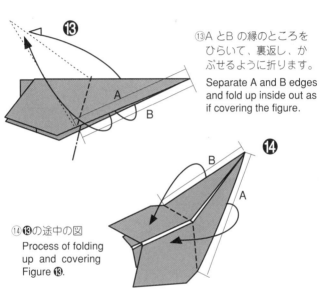

⑬AとBの縁のところを
　ひらいて、裏返し、か
　ぶせるように折ります。

Separate A and B edges
and fold up inside out as
if covering the figure.

⑭⑬の途中の図

Process of folding
up and covering
Figure ⑬.

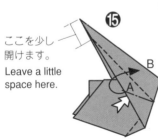

ここを少し
開けます。

Leave a little
space here.

⑮内側をひろげてAのところを
　Bのほうに引き寄せるように
　して折ります。
　反対側も同じです。

Pull A towards B and fold. Do
the same on the reverse side.

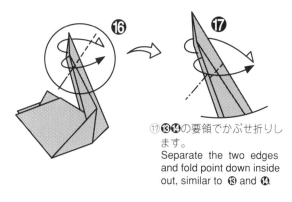

⑰⑬⑭の要領でかぶせ折りし
ます。
Separate the two edges
and fold point down inside
out, similar to ⑬ and ⑭

⑱内側に段に折ってくちばし
を作ります。
Form a beak by folding back
in an overlap.

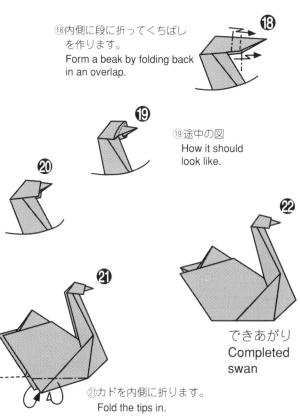

⑲途中の図
How it should
look like.

できあがり
Completed
swan

㉑カドを内側に折ります。
Fold the tips in.

ぞ　う　**Elephant**

今度は紙を2枚使って組み
合わせた折り紙です。まず
頭を作り、次に体を作りま
す。

An origami that is composed
of two separate parts. First
make the head, then the
body.

折り紙2枚　Two origami sheets

[頭]
Head

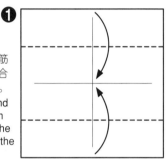

①はじめに縦、横に折り筋
　をつけてから、中心に合
　わせるように折ります。
　First fold vertically and
　horizontally to form
　creases. Then fold the
　two opposite edges to the
　center.

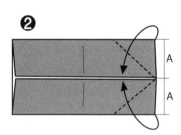

②Aの縁を中心に合わせる
　ように折ります。
　Bring edges A to the
　center and fold.

③Aの縁を中心に合わせる
　ように折ります。
　Bring edges A to the
　center and fold.

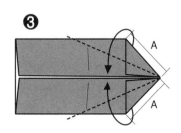

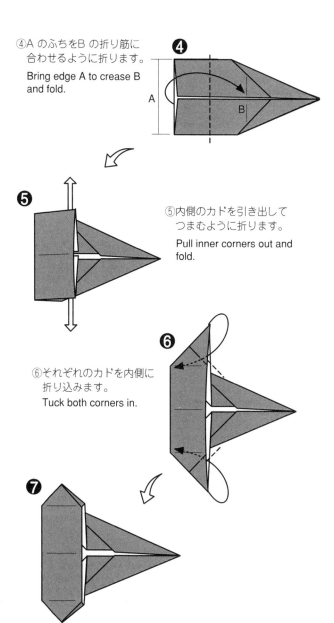

④AのふちをBの折り筋に
　合わせるように折ります。

Bring edge A to crease B
and fold.

A

B

⑤内側のカドを引き出して
　つまむように折ります。

Pull inner corners out and
fold.

⑥それぞれのカドを内側に
　折り込みます。
Tuck both corners in.

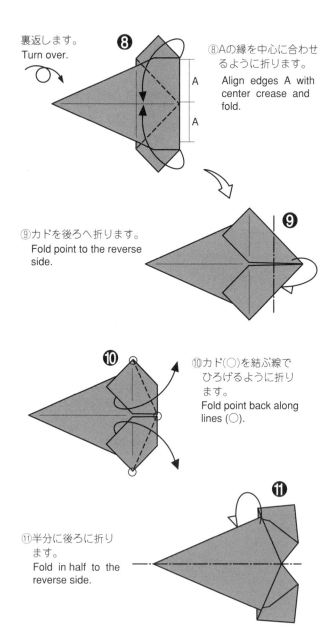

裏返します。
Turn over.

❽

⑧Aの縁を中心に合わせ
るように折ります。

Align edges A with
center crease and
fold.

A

A

⑨カドを後ろへ折ります。
Fold point to the reverse
side.

❾

❿

⑩カド(○)を結ぶ線で
ひろげるように折り
ます。
Fold point back along
lines (○).

⑪半分に後ろに折り
ます。
Fold in half to the
reverse side.

⓫

84

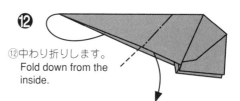

⑫ ⑫中わり折りします。
Fold down from the
inside.

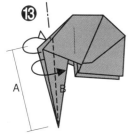

⑬ ⑬Aの縁をBの縁に合わせる
ようにして細く折ります。
Align edges A with edge B
and fold. Do the same on
the reverse side.

A

B

[頭]の
できあがり
Completion
of the head

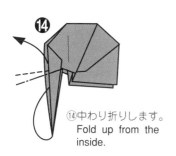

⑭ ⑭中わり折りします。
Fold up from the
inside.

⑮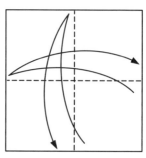

[体] Body

①縦、横半分に折り筋を
つけます。
Make creases vertically
and horizontally.

①

②つけた折り筋に合わせる
ようにして折り筋をつけ
ます。

Make creases on all four
sides up to the center fold.

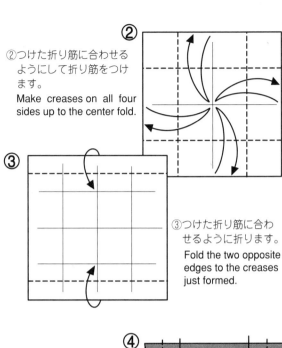

③つけた折り筋に合わ
せるように折ります。

Fold the two opposite
edges to the creases
just formed.

④②でつけた縦の折り筋の
1/2で段折りをします。

Fold up to the crease made
in ② and back again along
the crease line to form stairs.

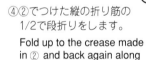

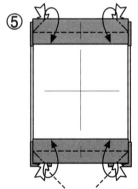

⑤内側をひろげて引き寄せるように
してつぶします。

While drawing the edges towards
the center, press down and fold
corners.

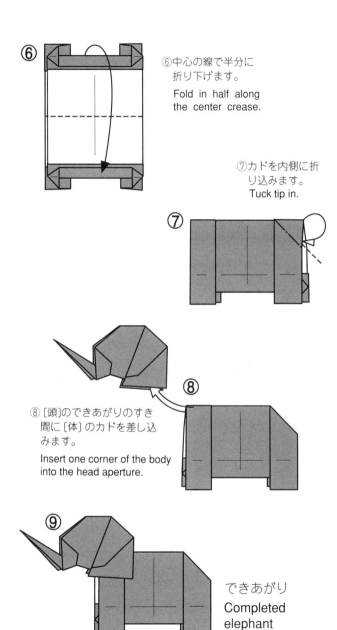

⑥ 中心の線で半分に
折り下げます。

Fold in half along
the center crease.

⑦ カドを内側に折
り込みます。
Tuck tip in.

⑧ [頭]のできあがりのすき
間に[体]のカドを差し込
みます。

Insert one corner of the body
into the head aperture.

できあがり
Completed
elephant

キリン　Giraffe

キリンも頭と体を別々に作
ります。体の部分が少しむ
ずかしいですよ。

This is also composed of two
separate parts, the head and
the body. The body is a little
difficult to make.

折り紙2枚
Two origami sheets

[頭]
Head

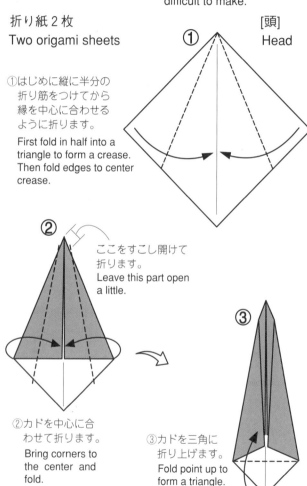

①はじめに縦に半分の
　折り筋をつけてから
　縁を中心に合わせる
　ように折ります。

First fold in half into a
triangle to form a crease.
Then fold edges to center
crease.

ここをすこし開けて
折ります。
Leave this part open
a little.

②カドを中心に合
　わせて折ります。
Bring corners to
the center and
fold.

③カドを三角に
　折り上げます。
Fold point up to
form a triangle.

④ 縦に半分に折ります。
Fold in half lengthwise.

⑤

⑤Aの縁をBの縁に合わせるように折ります。
Align edges A with edge B and fold. Do the same on the reverse side.

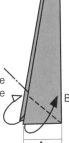

B

A

⑥

⑦中わり折りします。
Fold down from the inside.

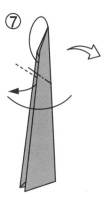

⑥カド(○)を結ぶ線でカドを内側に折り込みます。
Fold point to the inside along the line at points (○).

キリン　89

⑧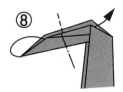

⑧カドが出るように中わり
折りします。

Fold up from the inside,
enough to form a point.

⑨

⑨カドを立てるように
中わり折りします。

Stand the point up by
folding down from the
inside.

⑩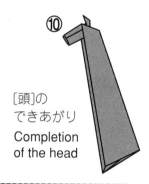

[頭]の
できあがり
Completion
of the head

---

❶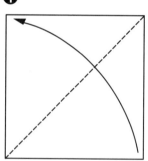

[体]　　　Body

①はじめに三角に折ります。
First fold into a triangle.

❷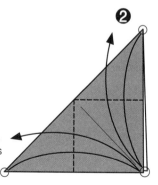

②カドとカド(○)を合わせて折
り筋をつけます。
Align the two opposite corners
with the point to form creases
and return to former position.

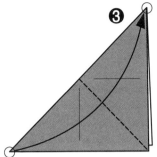

❸

③カドを合わせるように
三角に折ります。

Fold into a triangle by
matching corners (○)
together.

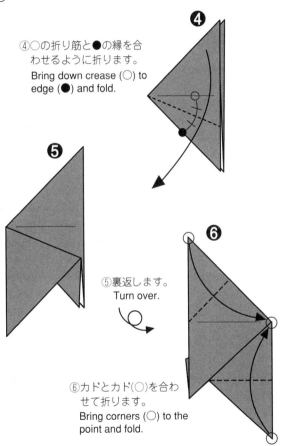

❹

④○の折り筋と●の縁を合
わせるように折ります。

Bring down crease (○) to
edge (●) and fold.

❺

⑤裏返します。
Turn over.

❻

⑥カドとカド(○)を合わ
せて折ります。

Bring corners (○) to the
point and fold.

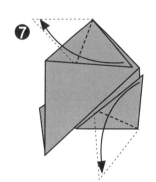

❼ ⑦それぞれカドを斜めに開く
ように折ります。
Swing corners out diagonally
and fold.

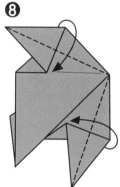

❽ ⑧それぞれカドが半分に
なるように折ります。
Fold both corners in
half.

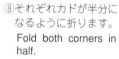

❾ ⑨カドとカド(○)を合わせる
ように折ります。
Bring points (○) together
and fold.

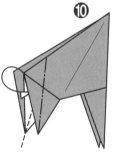

❿ ⑩カドを内側に折り
込みます。
Fold corners in.

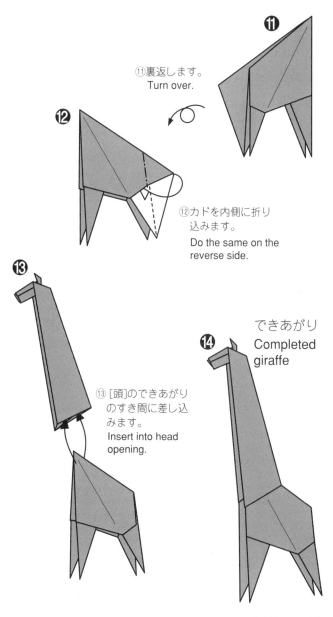

⑪裏返します。
Turn over.

⑪

⑫

⑫カドを内側に折り
込みます。
Do the same on the
reverse side.

⑬

⑬ [頭]のできあがり
のすき間に差し込
みます。
Insert into head
opening.

できあがり
⑭ Completed
giraffe

ライオン　Lion

これも紙を2枚使って作ります。1枚で頭と前足、もう1枚で胴と後足を作ります。

This is also made with two sheets of paper. The first sheet becomes the head and forelegs, and the second sheet becomes the torso and hind legs.

折り紙2枚
Two origami
sheets

[頭]
Head

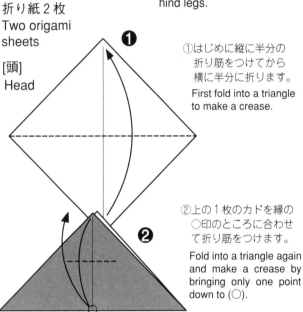

①はじめに縦に半分の折り筋をつけてから横に半分に折ります。
First fold into a triangle to make a crease.

②上の1枚のカドを縁の○印のところに合わせて折り筋をつけます。
Fold into a triangle again and make a crease by bringing only one point down to (○).

③縁を合わせるように折ります。
Bring corners up to the point and fold.

少し間を開けて折ります。
Leave a little space here.

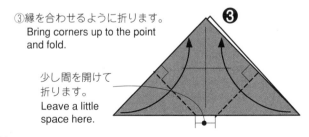

94

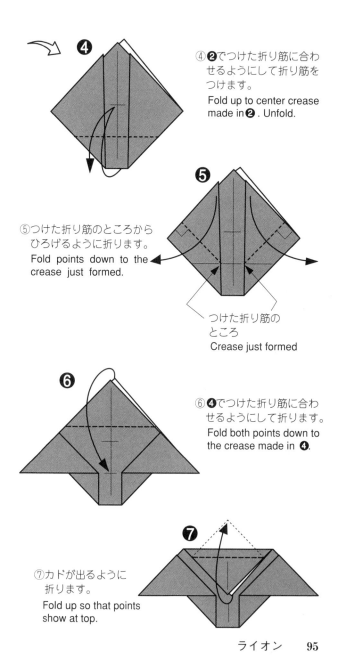

④ ④❷でつけた折り筋に合わ
せるようにして折り筋を
つけます。
Fold up to center crease
made in ❷. Unfold.

⑤ ⑤つけた折り筋のところから
ひろげるように折ります。
Fold points down to the
crease just formed.

つけた折り筋の
ところ
Crease just formed

⑥ ⑥❹でつけた折り筋に合わ
せるようにして折ります。
Fold both points down to
the crease made in ❹.

⑦ ⑦カドが出るように
折ります。
Fold up so that points
show at top.

ライオン　95

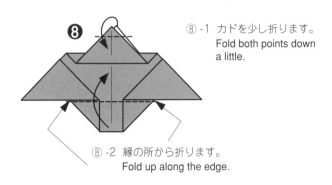

⑧ -1 カドを少し折ります。
Fold both points down
a little.

⑧ -2 縁の所から折ります。
Fold up along the edge.

⑨重なったカドのところで
折り筋をつけます。
Make a crease by folding
down at the overlap point.

重なったカドのところ
Overlap point

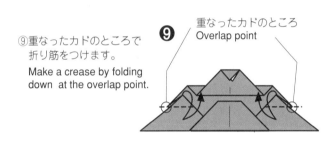

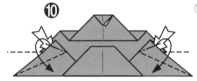

⑩矢印のところの内側を
ひろげてつぶすように
折ります。
Open at arrows, press
down and fold.

⑪カドとカドを合わ
せるようにして半
分に折ります。
Bring both points
together and fold.

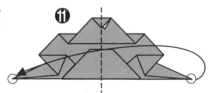

⑫ **⑫**鼻のところをつまんで引き下げるように折ります。
Lower nose down a little.

⑬カドを中わり折りで出すように折ります。
Fold point up from the inside.

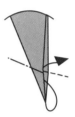

⑬

⑭同じようにしてカドを中わり折りで反対側に出すように折ります。
Then fold point in the opposite direction again from the inside.

⑭

〔前半身〕の
できあがり
Completion
of the head.

⑮カドを少し内側に折り込みます。反対側の足も同じに折ります。
Fold tip in a little. Fold the opposite leg in the same manner.

⑮

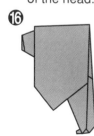

⑯

ライオン　**97**

[体] Body

① はじめに縦に半分の
折り筋をつけてから
縁を中心に合わせる
ように折ります。

First make a vertical
crease then bring
edges to the center
and fold.

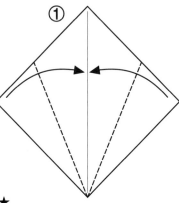

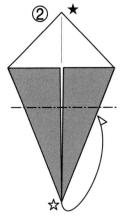

② ☆のカドを★のカドに
合わせるように後ろへ
折ります。

Fold to the reverse side
matching (☆) and (★).

③ ☆のカドを引き下げながら
つまむようにして折ります。

Make creases by aligning
edges with the center crease.
Unfold. Then lower (☆) flap.
Press down and fold.

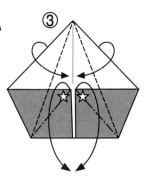

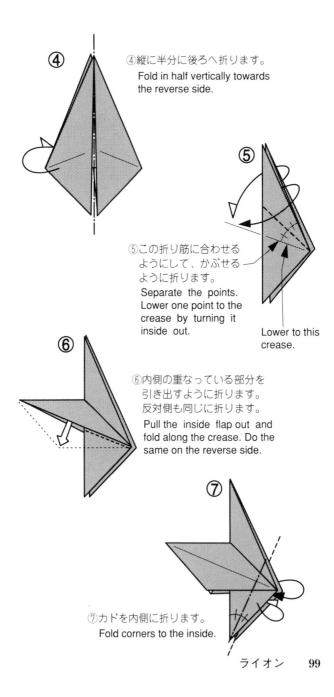

④

④縦に半分に後ろへ折ります。
Fold in half vertically towards
the reverse side.

⑤

⑤この折り筋に合わせる
ようにして、かぶせる
ように折ります。
Separate the points.
Lower one point to the
crease by turning it
inside out.

Lower to this
crease.

⑥

⑥内側の重なっている部分を
引き出すように折ります。
反対側も同じに折ります。
Pull the inside flap out and
fold along the crease. Do the
same on the reverse side.

⑦

⑦カドを内側に折ります。
Fold corners to the inside.

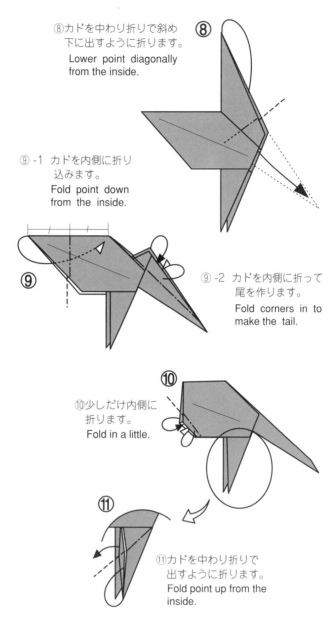

⑧カドを中わり折りで斜め
下に出すように折ります。
Lower point diagonally
from the inside.

⑨-1 カドを内側に折り
込みます。
Fold point down
from the inside.

⑨-2 カドを内側に折って
尾を作ります。
Fold corners in to
make the tail.

⑩少しだけ内側に
折ります。
Fold in a little.

⑪カドを中わり折りで
出すように折ります。
Fold point up from the
inside.

⑫同じようにしてカドを中わり折り
　で反対側に出すように折ります。

From the inside, fold tip in the
opposite direction so that it juts
out on the opposide side.

⑬もういちど同じようにして
　中わり折りで折ります。

Again, fold tip in the same
way in the opposite direction
from the inside.

⑭カドを少し内側に折り込みます。
　反対側の足も同じに折ります。

Fold tip a little to the inside.

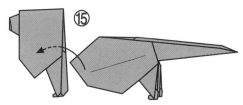

⑮前半身をすき間に差し込んで
　のりづけしてとめます。

Insert into the head and paste
together.

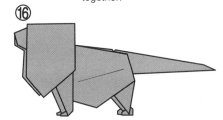

できあがり
Completed
lion

コアラ   Koala

大きさを変えたコアラを折
って、かわいいコアラの親
子を作ってみてください。

Vary the size of the paper to
make a cute mother-child pair.

折り紙2枚 Two origami sheets

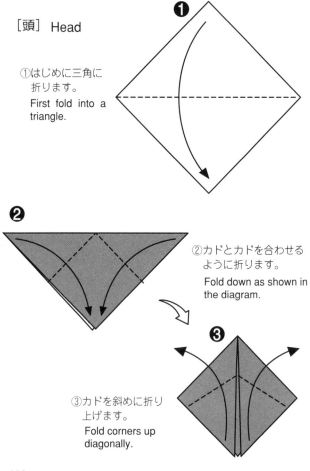

❶

[頭] Head

①はじめに三角に
　折ります。
　First fold into a
　triangle.

❷

②カドとカドを合わせる
　ように折ります。
　Fold down as shown in
　the diagram.

❸

③カドを斜めに折り
　上げます。
　Fold corners up
　diagonally.

④上のカドを○のカドの
　ところから折り下げま
　す。
Fold upper point down
at (○).

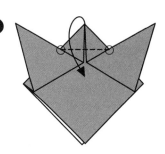

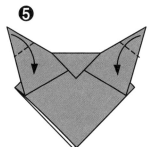

⑤それぞれカドを少し折り
　ます。
Fold tips down a little.

⑥○のカドのところで折って
　折り筋をつけます。
Fold down at (○) to form a
crease.

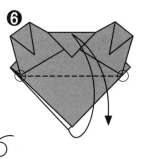

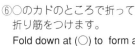

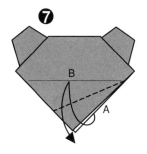

⑦縁を、つけた折り筋に
　合わせるように、もう
　一つ折り筋をつけます。
Make another crease
by folding edge A along
crease B.

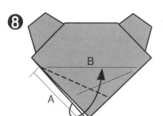

❽Aの縁をBの折り筋に合わせるように折ります。

Do the same on the other side.

❾上の1枚のカドを折り筋のついたカド（○）のところに折ります。

Fold upper point down to (○).

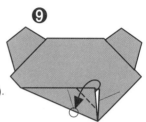

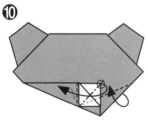

❿ついている折り筋を使って○のカドをつまむように折ります。

Pull (○) to the left bringing up the crease on the right at the same time. Fold down.

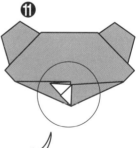

⑫内側をひろげてつぶすように折ります。

Open from the inside and fold by pressing down.

⑬それぞれカドを少し
　だけ後ろに折ります。
Fold tips in a little to
the reverse side.

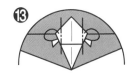

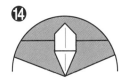

[頭]の
できあがり

Completion
of the head

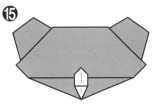

---

① 　　　　[体] Body

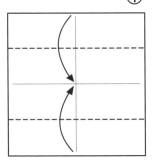

①はじめに縦、横半分に折
　り筋をつけてから、縁を
　中心に合わせるように折
　ります。
First fold in half vertically
and horizontally to form
creases. Then fold the
opposite edges to the
center.

②縁を中心に合わせる
　ように折ります。
Fold both edges to the
center.

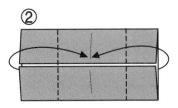

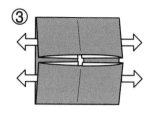

③ ③それぞれカドを引き出し
てつまむように折ります。

Pull corners out and fold
down.

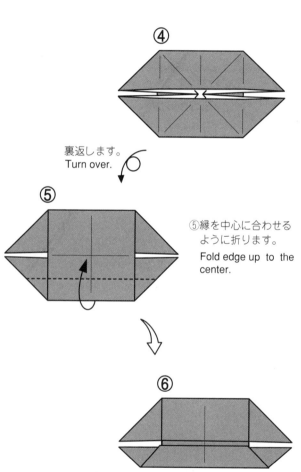

④

裏返します。
Turn over.

⑤ ⑤縁を中心に合わせる
ように折ります。

Fold edge up to the
center.

⑥

裏返します。
Turn over.

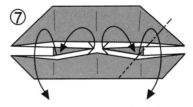

⑦下の縁を引き下げ、中心の
カドを左右に開くように折
ります。
Lower bottom flap and fold
center points outward to the
left and to the right.

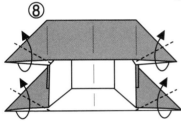

⑧それぞれカドを
斜めに折り上げ
ます。
Fold points up
diagonally.

⑨それぞれカドを斜めに
折り下げます。
Lower upper tips
diagonally.

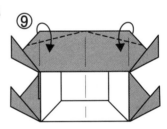

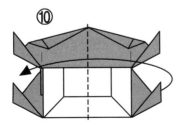

⑩縦に半分に折ります。
Fold in half vertically.

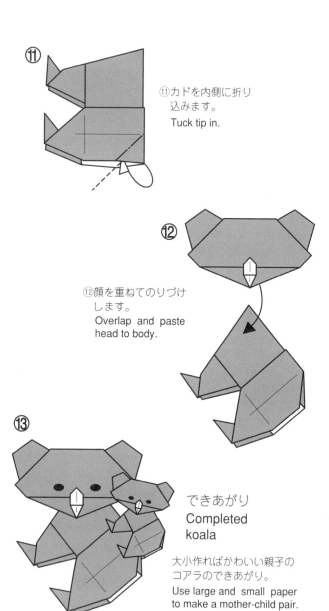

⑪カドを内側に折り
　込みます。
Tuck tip in.

⑫顔を重ねてのりづけ
　します。
Overlap and paste
head to body.

できあがり
Completed
koala

大小作ればかわいい親子の
コアラのできあがり。
Use large and small paper
to make a mother-child pair.

チューリップ **Tulip**

このチューリップは平面的な作品です。カードやはがきに貼ったりしても楽しめますね。

This is a flat tulip that can be pasted on cards or postcards. Send one and cheer a friend up.

折り紙 4 枚
Four origami sheets

[花]
Flower

①はじめに横に半分の折り筋をつけてから三角に折ります。
First make a horizontal crease then fold vertically into a triangle.

②カドとカド(○)を合わせて折り筋をつけます。
Bring lower corners (○) up to the point to make a crease.

③つぎにAの縁を❷でつけた折り筋Bに合わせて折ります。
Align edge A with crease B and fold.

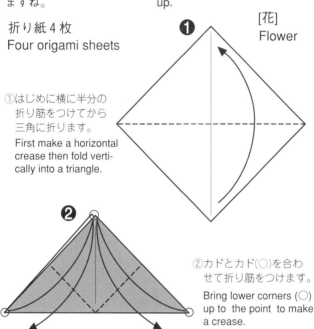

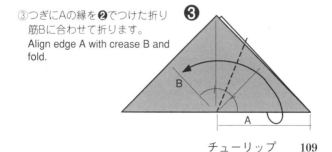

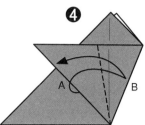

❹

④つぎにAの縁をBの縁に合わせて折り筋をつけます。

Next align edge A with edge B to make a crease.

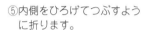

A   B

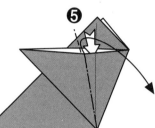

❺

⑤内側をひろげてつぶすように折ります。

Open up from the inside and fold by pressing down.

❻

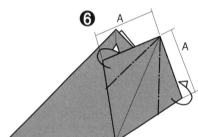

A

A

⑥つぎにAの縁を後ろの中心に合わせるように折ります。

Fold edges A to the reverse side to the center crease line.

❼

⑦反対側も❸〜❻と同じに折ります。

Follow the same procedure in ❸-❻ for the opposite corner.

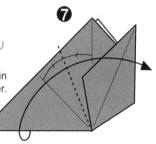

110

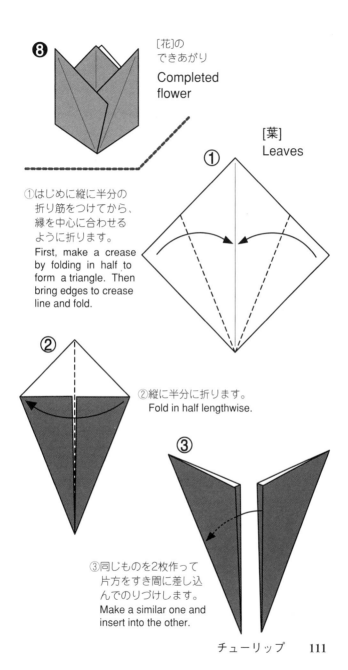

❽

[花]の
できあがり

Completed
flower

[葉]
Leaves

① はじめに縦に半分の
折り筋をつけてから、
縁を中心に合わせる
ように折ります。
First, make a crease
by folding in half to
form a triangle. Then
bring edges to crease
line and fold.

①

②縦に半分に折ります。
Fold in half lengthwise.

②

③

③同じものを2枚作って
片方をすき間に差し込
んでのりづけします。
Make a similar one and
insert into the other.

チューリップ　111

[くき] Stem

小さく切った紙を
使います。
Use a small piece
of paper.

❶ ①縦に半分に折り筋を
つけます。
Make a vertical crease.

❷ ②縁を中心の折り
筋に合わせるよ
うに折ります。
Bring the edges
to the center and
fold.

❸ ③半分に折ります。
Fold in half.

❹ ④それぞれのりづけ
します。
Paste the parts
together.

❺

できあがり
Completed
tulip

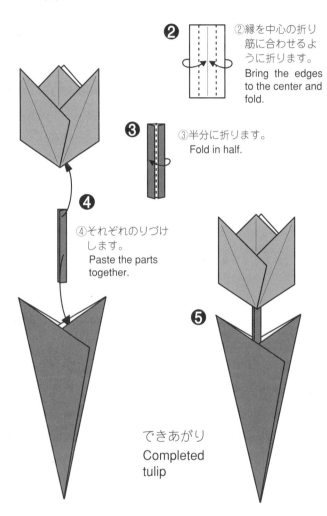

カーネーション Carnation

このカーネーションは両面
同じ色の薄手の紙で折ると
きれいです。

Use a thin sheet of paper the
same color on both sides to
create a beautiful flower.

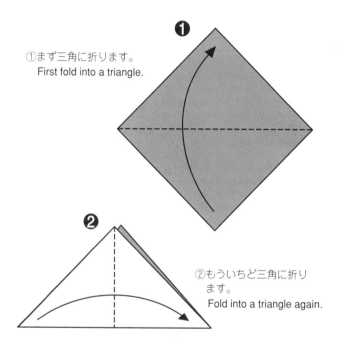

❶
①まず三角に折ります。
First fold into a triangle.

❷
②もういちど三角に折り
ます。
Fold into a triangle again.

❸
③内側をひろげて
つぶすように折
ります。
Spread open from
the inside and fold
by pressing down.

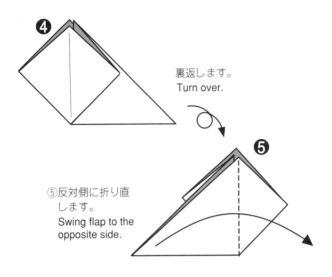

❹

裏返します。
Turn over.

⑤反対側に折り直
　します。
Swing flap to the
opposite side.

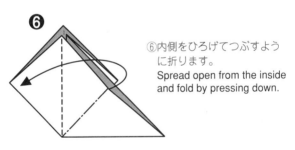

❺

❻

⑥内側をひろげてつぶすよう
　に折ります。
Spread open from the inside
and fold by pressing down.

❼

⑦ Aの縁をB の折り筋に
　合わせるように折りま
　す。
Bring edges A to crease
B and fold.

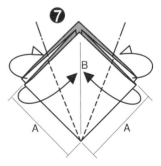

❽

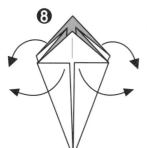

⑧しっかりと折り筋をつけて
　から戻します。

Press down firmly to make a
crease and return to former
position.

⑨つけた折り筋を使って内側を
　ひろげてつぶすように折りま
　す。

Using the crease just formed,
open up from the inside and
fold by pressing down.

❾

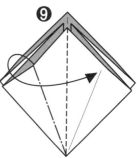

❿

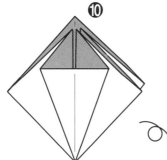

裏返します。
Turn over.

⓫

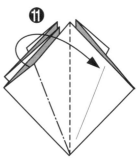

⑪つけた折り筋を使って内側を
　ひろげてつぶすように折りま
　す。

Using the crease just formed,
open up from the inside and
fold by pressing down.

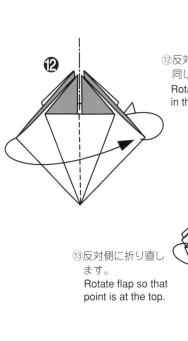

⑫反対側に折り直して残りも
同じに折ります。
Rotate flaps and fold all sides
in the same way.

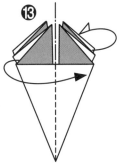

⑬反対側に折り直し
ます。
Rotate flap so that
point is at the top.

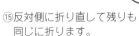

⑭カドを折り下げます。
Bring points down on
both sides.

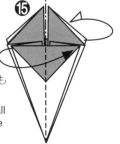

⑮反対側に折り直して残りも
同じに折ります。
Rotate flaps and bring all
points down in the same
manner.

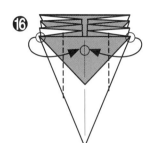

⑯カドを中心に折り
ます。
Bring points to the
center and fold.

⑰しっかりと折り筋をつけて
から戻します。
Press firmly to form a crease
and return to former position.

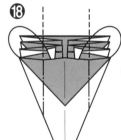

⑱つけた折り筋を使ってカドを
内側に折り込みます。
Using the crease just formed,
tuck points in.

⑲残りも同じに折り
ます。
Do the same to all
points.

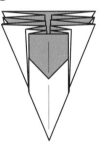

カーネーション　117

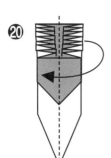

⑳縦に半分に折ります。
Fold in half vertically.

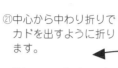

㉑中心から中わり折りで
　カドを出すように折り
　ます。

Bring up point from the
inside. Point should jut
out.

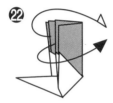

㉒中心のところから
　ひろげるように折
　ります。
Spread out from
the center.

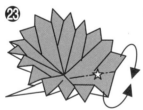

㉓☆印の折り筋を山折りに
　つけ直します。
Refold crease at (☆) by
raising it up.

できあがり
Completed
carnation

118

第 3 章
Chapter Three

楽しい飾り小物
Charming Decorative Accessories

鉛　筆　**Pencil**

たくさんの色で折って、色
鉛筆のセットを作ってもか
わいいですよ。

Make a color pencil set by
using different colored paper.

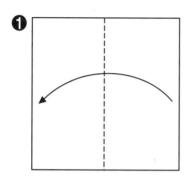

①はじめに縦に半分に折り
　ます。
First fold in half lengthwise.

②Aの縁をBの縁に合わせる
　ように折ります。

Align edges A with edge B
and fold. Return the reverse
side to its former position.

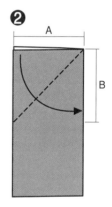

③Aの縁をBの縁に合わせるように
　後ろに折って折り筋をつけます。

On the reverse side, align edge
A with edge B and fold to make
a crease.

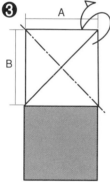

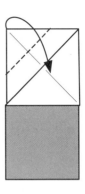

④カドが少し中心の縁より
　出るように折ります。

Fold down corner so that
it juts out a little from the
center.

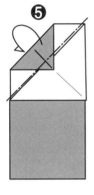

⑤縁に合わせて後ろに
　折ります。
Fold back at crease.

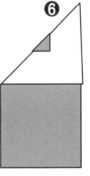

裏返します。
Turn over.

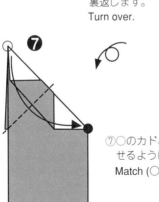

⑦○のカドと●のカドを合わ
　せるように折ります。
Match (○) and (●) and fold.

太い鉛筆のできあがり
Completion of a thick pencil

パンチなどで穴を開けてリボンを通
すと、かわいいしおりができます。
Punch a hole at the end and tie a
ribbon through to create a charming
bookmark.

細い鉛筆を作ります
To make a thin pencil

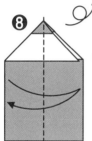

⑧半分に折り筋をつけ
ます。
Fold in half to make a
crease.

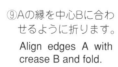

⑨Aの縁を中心Bに合わ
せるように折ります。
Align edges A with
crease B and fold.

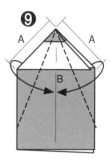

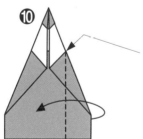

⑩このカドのところ
から折ります。
Fold at this point.

⑪反対側も同じように
折ります。
Fold the other side in
the same way.

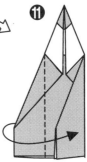

裏返します。
Turn over.

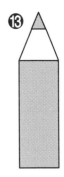

細い鉛筆の
できあがり

Completion of
a thin pencil

長方形の紙で折った
鉛筆

**A pencil made from
a rectangular piece
of paper**

長方形の紙で折ると
細長い鉛筆ができま
す。
A long, thin pencil can
be made by using a
rectangular piece of
paper.

シャツ　**Shirt**

ラッピングペーパーなどカラフルな紙を使うとかわいいものができます。

Use wrapping paper or a brightly colored paper to create a colorful shirt.

[シャツ1]
Shirt #1

①はじめに縦に半分に折って折り筋をつけます。
First fold in half lengthwise to form a crease.

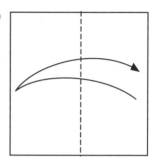

②つぎにAの縁を中心の折り筋Bに合わせて折ります。
Align edges A with center crease B and fold down.

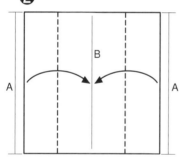

③半分に折って折り筋をつけます。
Fold in half to form a crease.

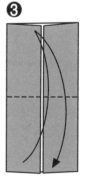

124

④中心(●)とカド(○)を結ぶ線で
　ひろげるように折ります。
Fold out along lines joining (●)
to (○).

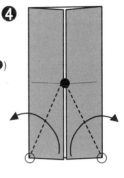

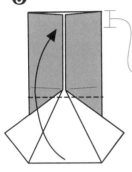

⑤上の衿になるところを少し幅を
　とって折り上げます。
Fold up leaving a little space at
the top for the collar.

⑥中心●とカド○を結ぶ
　線でひろげるように折
　ります。
Fold down along lines
joining (●) to (○).

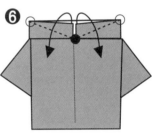

⑦裏返します。
Turn over.

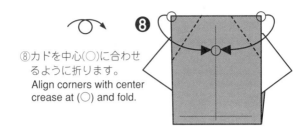

⑧カドを中心(○)に合わせ
るように折ります。
Align corners with center
crease at (○) and fold.

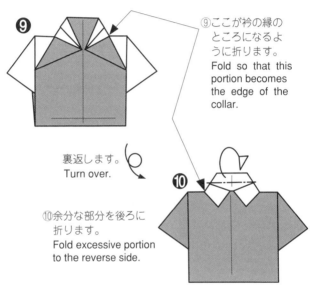

⑨ここが衿の縁の
ところになるよ
うに折ります。
Fold so that this
portion becomes
the edge of the
collar.

裏返します。
Turn over.

⑩余分な部分を後ろに
折ります。
Fold excessive portion
to the reverse side.

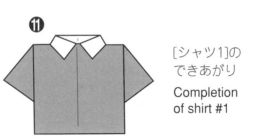

[シャツ1]の
できあがり
Completion
of shirt #1

126

[シャツ2]
Shirt #2

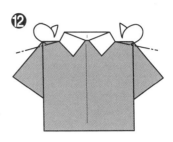

⑫肩のところのカドを少し
　だけ後ろに折ります。
　Fold shoulder tips back
　a little to the reverse side.

ここのカド

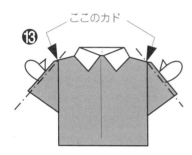

⑬肩のところのカドを
　少しだけ後ろに折り
　ます。
　Fold upper sleeve back
　a little.

[シャツ2]の
できあがり

Completion
of shirt #2

[工夫] An idea

いつもありがとう…………
……………………………

内側に、ちょっとしたメッ
セージを書いてから折って、
カードや手紙に使うことも
できます。

Write a short message and
fold. It can be used as a
card or a letter.

ワンピース　Dress

やさしくてかわいらしいワ
ンピースです。カードなど
に貼って、顔、手足をつけ
るとかわいい。

A charming dress that can be
pasted on a card. Draw in the
face and legs.

❶

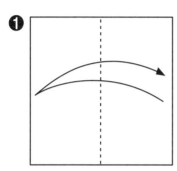

①はじめに縦に半分に折り筋
　をつけます。

First fold in half lengthwise
to form a crease.

②つぎに縁を中心に合わ
　せるように折ります。
Then bring edges to the
center crease and fold.

❷

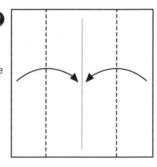

❸

③もういちど縁を中心に合わ
　せるように折ります。

Bring edges once more to
the center crease and fold.

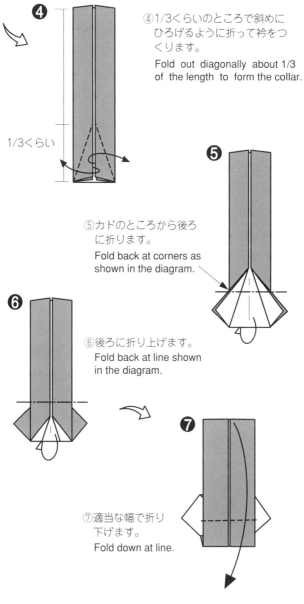

❹

④1/3くらいのところで斜めに
 ひろげるように折って衿をつ
 くります。

Fold out diagonally about 1/3
of the length to form the collar.

1/3くらい

❺

⑤カドのところから後ろ
 に折ります。

Fold back at corners as
shown in the diagram.

❻

⑥後ろに折り上げます。
Fold back at line shown
in the diagram.

❼

⑦適当な幅で折り
 下げます。
Fold down at line.

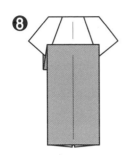

❽

裏返します。
Turn over.

❾

⑨重なっている部分を引き離す
ようにしてひろげます。
Spread open the overlapping
portion.

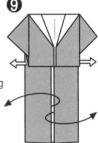

❿

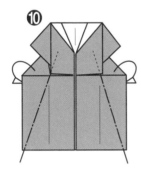

⑩斜めに後ろに折ります。
Fold diagonally to the
reverse side.

⓫

できあがり
Completed
dress

ハート Heart

簡単ですっきりしたデザインのハート。バレンタインの時にいかがですか。

A refreshingly simple design. Why not make one for Valentine's Day?

①はじめに縦に半分の折り筋をつけてから、カドとカドを合わせるように折ります。

First fold into a triangle to make a crease.

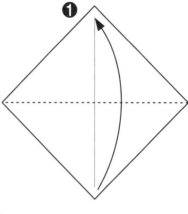

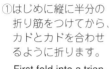

②カドに合わせて折り筋をつけます。

Bring corners up to top point and fold to form a crease. Return to former position.

③下の縁より少し上のところにカドを折り下げます。

Fold point down at a place just before it touches the bottom edge.

ここを少し開けます。
Leave a little space open here.

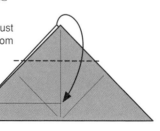

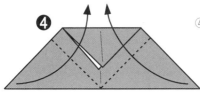

❹ ④❷でつけた折り筋で
カドを折り上げます。
Fold corners up at
creases made in ❷.

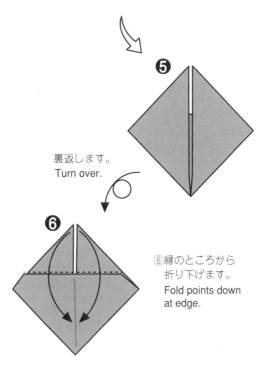

❺

裏返します。
Turn over.

❻ ⑥縁のところから
折り下げます。
Fold points down
at edge.

⑦内側をひろげてつぶす
ように折ります。
Open from the inside
and fold by pressing
down.

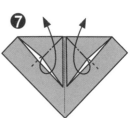

❼

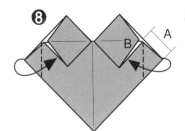

⑧Aの縁をBの縁に合わせる
　ように折ります。

Align edges A with edges
B and fold.

⑨上のカドを少し
　折り下げます。
Fold the tips
down a little.

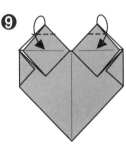

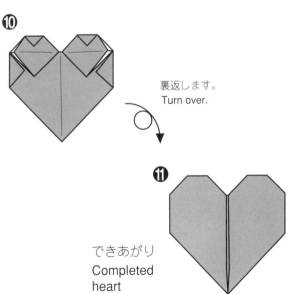

裏返します。
Turn over.

できあがり
Completed
heart

ベビーシューズ **Baby Shoes**

いかにもかわいらしいくつ
です。出産祝いのプレゼン
トに添えてみてはいかがで
すか。

Irresistible! Attach it on to a
present for baby.

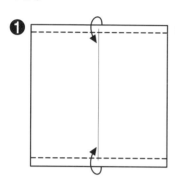

①はじめに縦に半分に折って
　折り筋をつけてから上下の
　縁を少しだけ折ります。

First fold in half vertically to
form a crease. Then fold
the upper and lower edges
in a little.

②つぎに横に半分に折って
　折り筋をつけます。

Fold lengthwise to form a
crease.

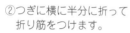
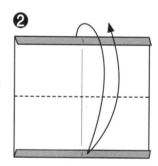

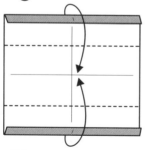

③縁をつけた折り筋に合わ
　せるように折ります。

Bring the rimmed edges to
the center crease and fold.

134

❹

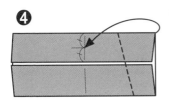

④カドを1/2の幅のところの
　折り筋の上に合わせるよう
　に折ります。

Bring corner to one half of
the crease and fold.

❺

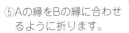

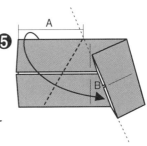

⑤Aの縁をBの縁に合わせ
　るように折ります。

Align edge A with edge
B and fold.

❻

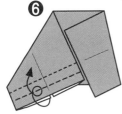

⑥縁を巻くように2回
　折ります。

Fold lower edge up
twice.

❼

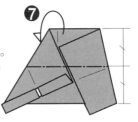

⑦半分で後ろに折ります。

Fold in half lengthwise
to the reverse side.

❽

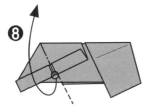

⑧中心(○)のところをつまむ
　ように引き上げます。

Bring (○) up and fold as if
covering the figure.

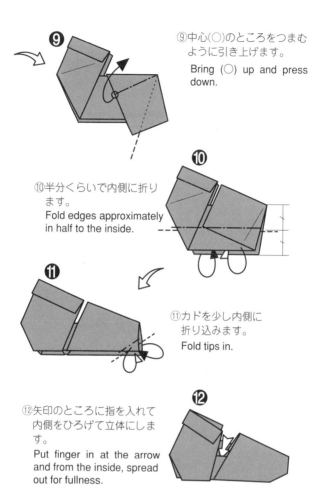

⑨中心(○)のところをつまむ
ように引き上げます。

Bring (○) up and press
down.

⑩半分くらいで内側に折り
ます。
Fold edges approximately
in half to the inside.

⑪カドを少し内側に
折り込みます。
Fold tips in.

⑫矢印のところに指を入れて
内側をひろげて立体にしま
す。
Put finger in at the arrow
and from the inside, spread
out for fullness.

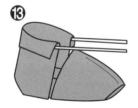

⑬適当な紐をすき間に
通して結びます。

Tie a string around
the rim.

⑭同じものを２つ作り
ます。

Make a matching pair.

できあがり
Completed
shoe

[工夫]
Great
Ideas

包装紙などを使っても
かわいいものができま
す。

Use wrapping paper to
create variety.

プレゼントを入れて
心の通う入れ物に。

Put a present in for a
heartwarming gift.

大きめのものを作るときには
少し厚手の紙を使います。

Use thicker paper for a larger
shoe.

小さめに作って
マスコットに

Make it smaller
for use as a
charm.

指　輪　Ring

7.5〜8センチぐらいの紙で作ると指に合います。中心にホイル紙などを貼るときれいです。

Use a 7.5-8 cm (2.5-3 inch) square sheet of paper to make a ring to fit your finger. Apply foil on the center and make it glitter.

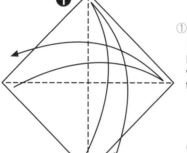

①はじめに縦、横三角に折り筋をつけます。

First fold into a triangle vertically and horizontally to form creases.

②カドを中心に合わせるようにして折り筋をつけます。

Bring both corners to the center and fold to form a crease.

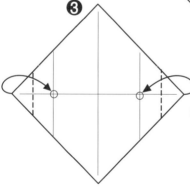

③つけた印(○)にカドを合わせるようにして折ります。

Fold both corners to (○).

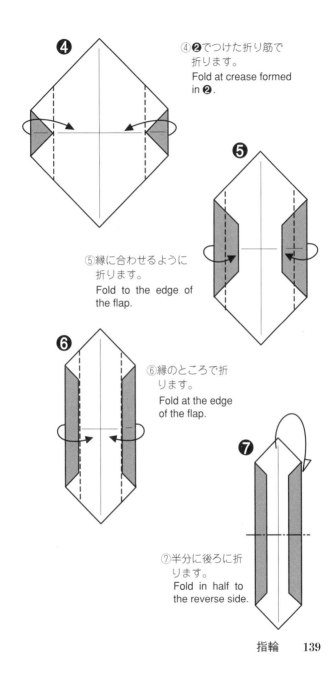

❹⓶でつけた折り筋で
折ります。
Fold at crease formed
in ⓶.

⑤縁に合わせるように
折ります。
Fold to the edge of
the flap.

⑥縁のところで折
ります。
Fold at the edge
of the flap.

⑦半分に後ろに折
ります。
Fold in half to
the reverse side.

指輪　139

⑧

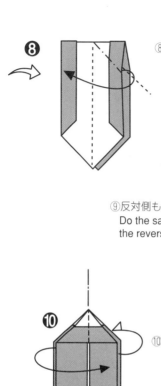

⑧内側をひろげてつぶすように
　折ります。
　Spread out from the inside and
　fold.

⑨

⑨反対側も同じ。
Do the same on
the reverse side.

⑩

⑩それぞれ反対側に
　折りずらします。
　Swing sides once
　around.

⑪それぞれ縁を中心に合わ
　せるように折ります。
　Bring edges to the center
　and fold. Do the same on
　the reverse side.

⑪

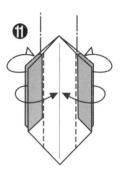

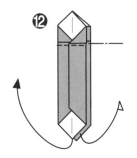

⑫ひろげます。
Open.

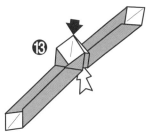

⑬内側をひろげて立体的にします。
Spread out from the inside to create fullness.

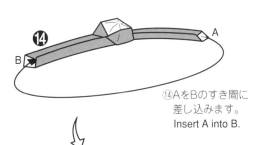

A

B

⑭AをBのすき間に差し込みます。
Insert A into B.

⑮縁を少し内側に折って細くします。
Make ring band narrower by folding to the inner side.

できあがり
Completed ring

くつした   Socks

クリスマス飾りにとても重宝な作品です。また、カードに貼ってもいいですね。

A useful item for Christmas. It can also be used as decoration on a card.

❶

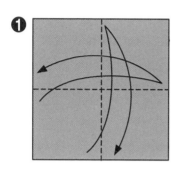

①はじめに縦、横半分に折り筋をつけます。
Make creases by folding vertically and horizontally.

❷

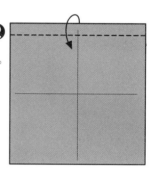

②縁を少しだけ折り下げます。
Fold the edge down a little.

❸

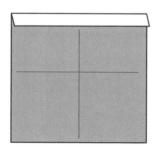

142

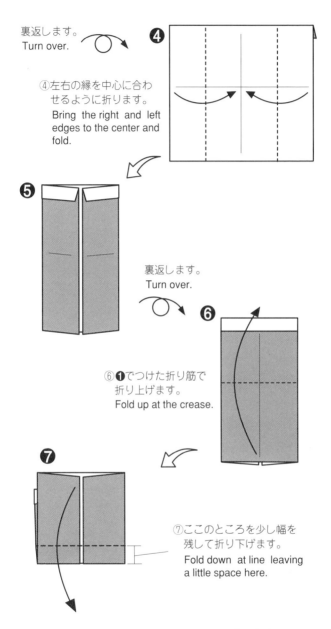

裏返します。
Turn over.

④左右の縁を中心に合わ
せるように折ります。
Bring the right and left
edges to the center and
fold.

裏返します。
Turn over.

⑥❶でつけた折り筋で
折り上げます。
Fold up at the crease.

⑦ここのところを少し幅を
残して折り下げます。
Fold down at line leaving
a little space here.

くつした   143

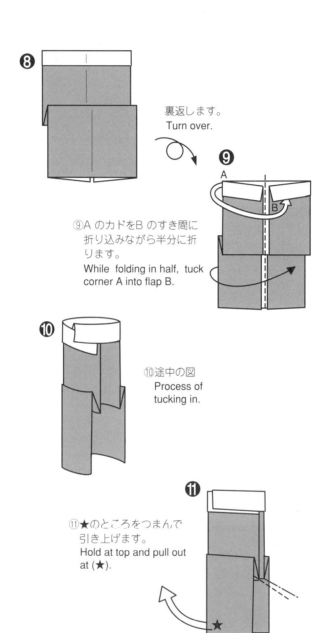

❽

裏返します。
Turn over.

❾

A

B

⑨A のカドをB のすき間に
　折り込みながら半分に折
　ります。
　While folding in half, tuck
　corner A into flap B.

❿

⑩途中の図
　Process of
　tucking in.

⓫

⑪★のところをつまんで
　引き上げます。
　Hold at top and pull out
　at (★).

★

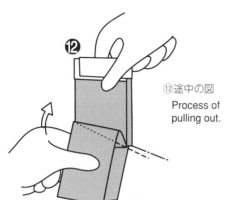

⑫途中の図
Process of
pulling out.

⑬カドを少し内側に
折り込みます。
Tuck in tip.

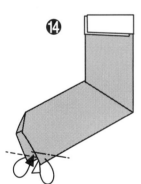

⑭カドを少し内側に折り
ます。
Tuck in lower tips.

できあがり
Completion
of sock

クリスマスの飾りだけでなく、リボンをあしらってカードを作ってみてはいかがですか。

This can be used not only as a Christmas decoration but also on a card. Tie a ribbon through it for added effect.

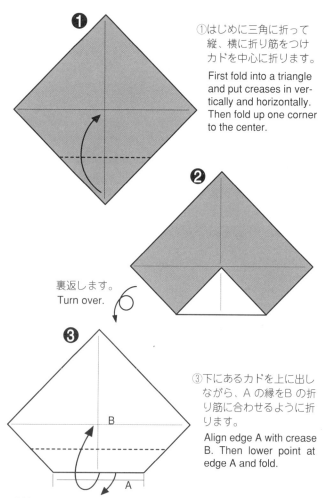

❶

①はじめに三角に折って縦、横に折り筋をつけカドを中心に折ります。

First fold into a triangle and put creases in vertically and horizontally. Then fold up one corner to the center.

❷

裏返します。
Turn over.

❸

③下にあるカドを上に出しながら、Aの縁をBの折り筋に合わせるように折ります。

Align edge A with crease B. Then lower point at edge A and fold.

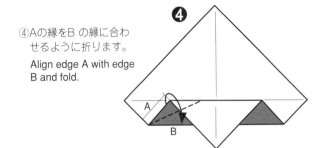

④Aの縁をB の縁に合わ
　せるように折ります。

Align edge A with edge
B and fold.

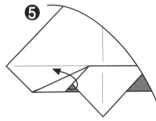

⑤しっかりと折り筋を
　つけてから戻します。

Press down firmly to
form a crease and
return to former po-
sition.

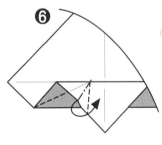

⑥つけた折り筋を使って内側を
　ひろげて、左に引き寄せるよ
　うに折ります。

Using the crease just formed,
open up from the inside and
fold down.

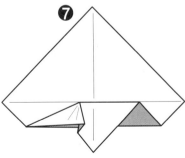

⑦反対側も④～⑥と
　同じに折ります。

Fold the other side
the same way as in
④-⑥.

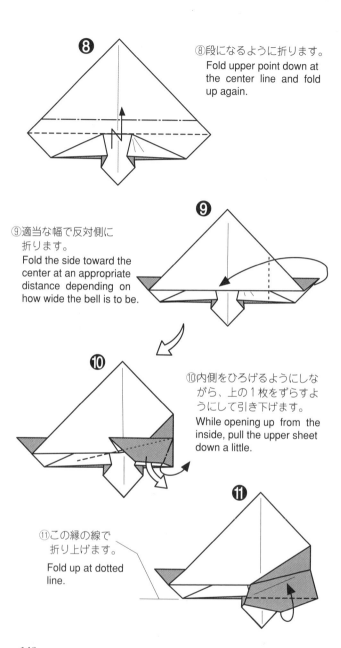

❽

⑧段になるように折ります。
Fold upper point down at the center line and fold up again.

⑨適当な幅で反対側に折ります。
Fold the side toward the center at an appropriate distance depending on how wide the bell is to be.

❾

❿

⑩内側をひろげるようにしながら、上の1枚をずらすようにして引き下げます。
While opening up from the inside, pull the upper sheet down a little.

⓫

⑪この縁の線で折り上げます。
Fold up at dotted line.

⑫反対側も❾〜⓫と同じに
折ります。

Do the same for the other
side as shown in ❾-⓫.

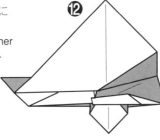

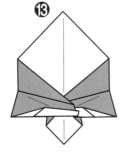

裏返します。
Turn over.

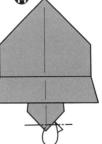

⑭下のカドを少しだけ後ろ
に折ります。

Fold bottom tip back a
little to the reverse side.

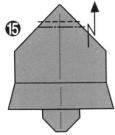

⑮ 段になるように折り
ます。

Make a staircase fold.

できあがり
Completed
bell

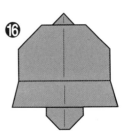

星　**Star**

折り紙の中で最もやさしい
星です。壁面飾りから、ク
リスマス飾り、カードにと
便利です。

One of the easiest origami to
make. Use as a wall decoration, a Christmas decoration
or as an ornament on a card.

折り紙3枚
Three origami
sheets

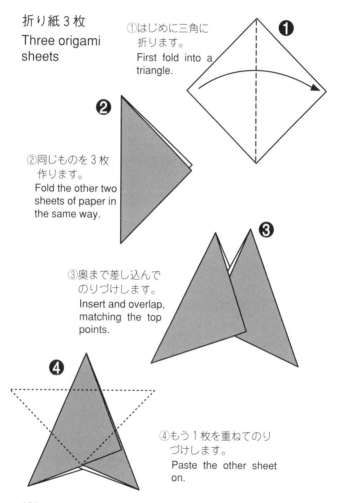

①はじめに三角に
折ります。
First fold into a
triangle.

❶

❷

②同じものを3枚
作ります。
Fold the other two
sheets of paper in
the same way.

❸

③奥まで差し込んで
のりづけします。
Insert and overlap,
matching the top
points.

❹

④もう1枚を重ねてのり
づけします。
Paste the other sheet
on.

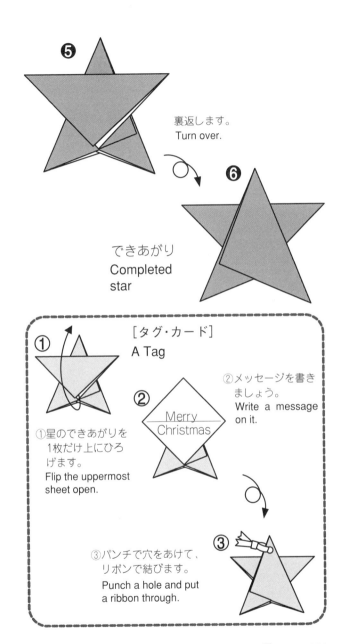

❺

裏返します。
Turn over.

❻

できあがり
Completed
star

[タグ・カード]
A Tag

①

②メッセージを書き
ましょう。
Write a message
on it.

②

Merry
Christmas

①星のできあがりを
1枚だけ上にひろ
げます。
Flip the uppermost
sheet open.

③パンチで穴をあけて、
リボンで結びます。
Punch a hole and put
a ribbon through.

③

星の子　**Star Kids**

やさしい星にかわいい顔を
つけて星の子のできあがり。
壁面に、クリスマスツリー
にどうぞ。

Make a star kid by drawing
a cute face on a star. Use as
a wall decoration or on a
Christmas tree.

折り紙5枚
Five origami
sheets

[顔]
Face

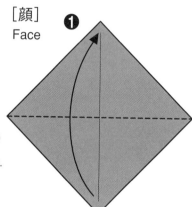

①はじめに縦に半分に
　折り筋をつけてから
　横に半分に折ります。
First fold vertically to
form a crease. Then
fold in half horizontally.

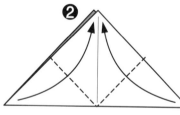

②カドとカドを合わせる
　ように折ります。
Bring corners to the
top point and fold.

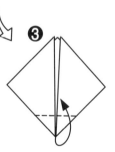

③カドを少し上に折り
　ます。
Fold bottom point up
a little.

❹

裏返します。
Turn over.

[顔]の
できあがり
Completion
of the face

❺

151ページの星を体として
使います。体(星)と顔、帽
子の紙の大きさは同じです。

Use the star shown on p.151
for the body. The body (star),
face and hat are all made
from the same sized paper.

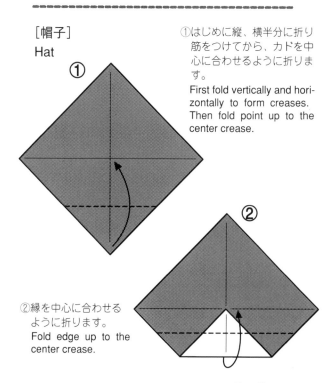

[帽子]
Hat

①

①はじめに縦、横半分に折り
　筋をつけてから、カドを中
　心に合わせるように折りま
　す。

First fold vertically and horizontally to form creases.
Then fold point up to the
center crease.

②

②縁を中心に合わせる
　ように折ります。
Fold edge up to the
center crease.

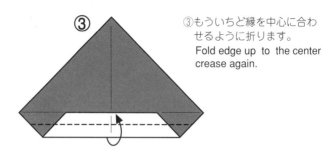

③もういちど縁を中心に合わ
　せるように折ります。
　Fold edge up to the center
　crease again.

④折り筋のところ
　で折ります。
　Fold at crease.

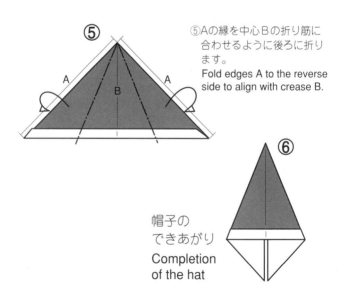

⑤Aの縁を中心Bの折り筋に
　合わせるように後ろに折り
　ます。
　Fold edges A to the reverse
　side to align with crease B.

帽子の
できあがり
Completion
of the hat

[組み合わせ方] Combine

①帽子のすき間に顔の上の
　カドを差し込んでのりづ
　けします。
　Insert upper point of face
　into hat opening and paste.

❷

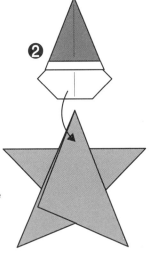

②つぎに同じ大きさの紙で
　折った体となる星に、組
　んだ顔と帽子を重ねての
　りづけします。
　Place face and hat pair on
　star body made from the
　same sized paper.

❸

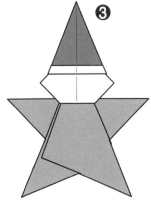

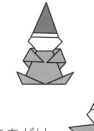

できあがり
Completion
of a star kid

サンタクロース Santa Claus

おひげの優しいサンタさん。おひげがもこもこした感じになるように切ってあげてください。

Jovial Santa and his beard. Cut it so that Santa will have a full beard.

折り紙2枚
Two origami sheets

①はじめに縦に半分の折り筋をつけてから、縁を中心に合わせるように折ります。

First fold into a triangle to make a crease. Then align edges with crease and fold.

[ひげ]
Beard

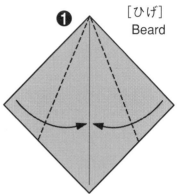

❶

❷

②しっかりと折り筋をつけてから戻します。
Press down firmly and return to former position.

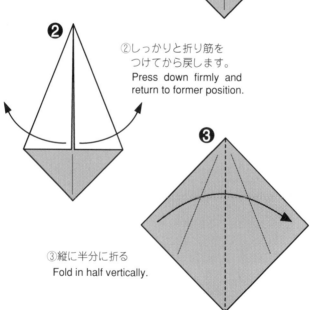

❸

③縦に半分に折る
Fold in half vertically.

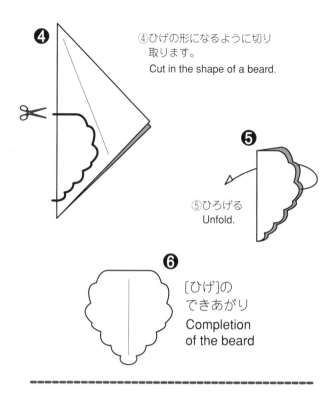

❹
④ひげの形になるように切り取ります。
Cut in the shape of a beard.

❺
⑤ひろげる
Unfold.

❻
[ひげ]の
できあがり
Completion
of the beard

[頭]
Head

①
①はじめに縦に半分の折り筋をつけてから、縁を中心に合わせるように折ります。
First fold into a triangle to make a crease. Then bring edges to center crease and fold.

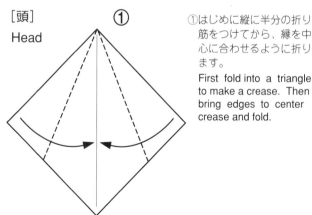

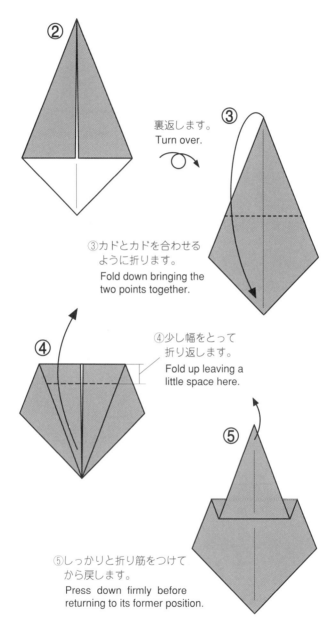

②

裏返します。
Turn over.

③

③カドとカドを合わせる
ように折ります。
Fold down bringing the
two points together.

④

④少し幅をとって
折り返します。
Fold up leaving a
little space here.

⑤

⑤しっかりと折り筋をつけて
から戻します。
Press down firmly before
returning to its former position.

158

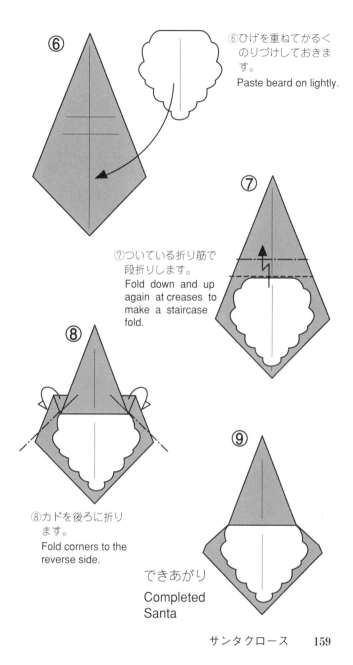

⑥ひげを重ねてかるく
のりづけしておきま
す。

Paste beard on lightly.

⑦ついている折り筋で
段折りします。
Fold down and up
again at creases to
make a staircase
fold.

⑧カドを後ろに折り
ます。
Fold corners to the
reverse side.

できあがり
Completed
Santa

英語で折り紙
Origami in English

1996年 4 月19日　第 1 刷発行
1997年10月28日　第10刷発行

著　者　山口　真

発行者　野間佐和子

発行所　講談社インターナショナル株式会社

　　　　〒112　東京都文京区音羽　1-17-14

　　　　電話：03-3944-6493（編集）

　　　　　　　03-3944-6492（営業）

印刷所　大日本印刷株式会社

製本所　株式会社　堅省堂

講談社バイリンガル・ブックス

英語で読んでも面白い！

- 楽しく読めて自然に英語が身に付くバイリンガル表記
- 実用から娯楽まで読者の興味に応える多彩なテーマ
- 重要単語、表現法が一目で分かる段落対応レイアウト

46判変型 (113 x 188 mm) 仮製

英語で話す「日本」Q & A
Talking About Japan Q & A

講談社インターナショナル ［編］　　　　　　320ページ　ISBN 4-7700-2026-0

外国の人と話すとき、必ず出てくる話題は「日本」のこと。でも英語力よりも前に困るのは、日本について知らないことがいっぱいという事実です。モヤモヤの知識をスッキリさせてくれる「日本再発見」の書。

英語で話す「アメリカ」Q & A
Talking About the USA Q & A

賀川　洋 ［著］　　　　　　　　　　　　　320ページ　ISBN 4-7700-2005-8

仕事でも留学でも遊びでも、アメリカ人と交際するとき、知っておくと役に立つ「アメリカ小事典」。アメリカ人の精神と社会システムにポイントをおいた解説により、自然、歴史、政治、文化、そして人をバイリンガルで紹介します。

英語で話す「世界」Q & A
Talking About the World Q & A

講談社インターナショナル ［編］　　　　　　320ページ　ISBN 4-7700-2006-6

今、世界にはいくつの国家があるか、ご存じですか？　対立をはらみながらも、急速に1つの運命共同体になっていく「世界」——外国の人と話すとき知らなければならない「世界」に関する国際人必携の「常識集」です。

英語で読む日本史
Japanese History: 11 Experts Reflect on the Past

「英文日本大事典」［編］ 　　　　　　　　　　224ページ　ISBN 4-7700-2024-4

11人の超一流ジャパノロジストたちが英語で書き下ろした日本全史。外国人の目から見た日本史はどういうものか、また、日本の歴史事項を英語で何と表現するのか。新しい視点が想像力をかき立てます。

英語で話す「日本の謎」Q & A　外国人が聞きたがる100のWHY
100 Tough Questions for Japan

板坂 元［監修］ 　　　　　　　　　　　　240ページ　ISBN 4-7700-2091-0

なぜ、結婚式は教会で、葬式はお寺でなんてことができるの？　なぜ、大人までがマンガを読むの？　なぜ、時間とお金をかけてお茶を飲む練習をするの？──こんな外国人の問いをつきつめてゆくと、日本文化の核心が見えてきます。

英語で話す「日本の心」　和英辞典では引けないキーワード197
Keys to the Japanese Heart and Soul

「英文日本大事典」［編］ 　　　　　　　　320ページ　ISBN 4-7700-2082-1

一流のジャパノロジスト53人が解説した「日本の心」を知るためのキーワード集。「わび」「さび」「義理人情」「甘え」「根回し」「談合」「みそぎ」など、日本人特有な「心の動き」を外国人に説明するための強力なツールです。

英語で話す「日本の文化」
Japan as I see It

NHK国際局文化プロジェクト［編］　ダン・ケニー［訳］　196ページ　ISBN 4-7700-2197-6

金田一春彦、遠藤周作、梅原猛、平川祐弘、西堀栄三郎、鯖田豊之、野村万作、井上靖、小松左京、中根千枝の１０人が、日本文化の「謎」を解く。NHKの国際放送で２１の言語で放送され、分かりやすいと世界中で大好評。

ニッポン不思議発見！　日本文化を英語で語る５０の名エッセイ集
Discover Japan: Words, Customs and Concept

日本文化研究所［編］　松本道弘［訳］ 　　　260ページ　ISBN 4-7700-2142-9

絶望的な場合ですら、日本人は「そこをなんとか」という言葉を使って、相手に甘えようとする……こんな指摘をうけると、いかに日本人は独特なものの考え方をしているか分かります。あなたも“不思議”を発見してみませんか。

ニッポン見聞録　大好きな日本人に贈る　新・開国論
Heisei Highs and Lows

トム・リード［著］ 　　　　　　　　　　　216ページ　ISBN 4-7700-2092-9

国際化の進む日本ですが、アメリカのジャーナリストが鋭い目と耳で浮き彫りにしたニッポンの姿は、驚くほど平穏でいとおしく、恥ずかしいくらい強欲で無知なものでした。トムが大好きな日本人へ贈る新・開国論。

「Japan」クリッピング　ワシントンポストが書いた「日本」
Views of Japan from the Washington Post Newsroom

東郷茂彦［著］ 　　　　　　　　　　　　256ページ　ISBN 4-7700-2023-6

アメリカの世論をリードするワシントン・ポストに書かれた「Japan」……政治、外交、経済、社会のジャンルで取り上げられた日本の姿を、国際ジャーナリストが解説し、その背後にある問題点を浮き彫りにする一冊。

誤解される日本人　外国人がとまどう41の疑問
The Inscrutable Japanese

メリディアン・リソーシス・アソシエイツ［編］ 賀川 洋［著］　　　224ページ　ISBN 4-7700-2129-1

あなたのちょっとした仕草や表情が大きな誤解を招いているかもしれません。「日本人はどんなときに誤解を受けるのか？」そのメカニズムを解説し、「どのように外国人に説明すればよいか」最善の解決策を披露します。

ビジュアル 英語で読む日本国憲法
The Constitution of Japan

「英文日本大百科事典」［編］　　　　　　　　　　　208ページ　ISBN 4-7700-2191-7

難しいと思っていた「日本国憲法」も、英語で読むと不思議とよく分かります。日本国憲法を、59点の写真を使って、バイリンガルで分かりやすく解説しました。条文中に出てくる難解な日本語には、ルビや説明が付いています。

イラスト 日本まるごと事典
Japan at a Glance

インターナショナル・インターンシップ・プログラムズ［著］　　　248ページ（2色刷）ISBN 4-7700-2080-5

1000点以上のイラストを使って日本のすべてを紹介──自然、文化、社会はもちろんのこと、折り紙の折り方、着物の着方から、ナベで米を炊く方法や「あっちむいてホイ」の遊び方まで国際交流に必要な知識とノウハウを満載。

英語で折り紙
Origami in English

山口 真［著］　　　　　　　　　　　　　　　　160ページ　ISBN 4-7700-2027-9

たった一枚の紙から無数の造形が生まれ出る‥‥外国の人たちは、その面白さに目を見張ります。折るとき、英語で説明できるようにバイリンガルにしました。ホームステイ、留学、海外駐在に必携の一冊です。

英語で日本料理
100 Recipes from Japanese Cooking

辻調理師専門学校　畑耕一郎、近藤一樹［著］
　　　　　　　　　　　　　　　268ページ（カラー口絵16ページ）　ISBN 4-7700-2079-1

外国の人と親しくなる最高の手段は、日本料理を作ってあげること、そしてその作り方を教えてあげることです。代表的な日本料理100品の作り方を、外国の計量法も入れながら、バイリンガルで分かりやすく解説しました。

アメリカ日常生活のマナーQ & A
Do As Americans Do

ジェームス・M・バーダマン，倫子・バーダマン［著］　　　256ページ　ISBN 4-7700-2128-3

"How do you do?" に "How do you do?" と答えてはいけないということ、ご存知でしたか？　日本では当たり前と思われていたことがマナー違反だったのです。旅行で、駐在で、留学でアメリカに行く人必携のマナー集。

日米比較 冠婚葬祭のマナー
Do It Right: Japanese & American Social Etiquette

ジェームス・M・バーダマン, 倫子・バーダマン [著]　　184ページ　ISBN 4-7700-2025-2

アメリカでは結婚式や葬式はどのように行われるのか？　お祝いや香典は？……そしてアメリカの人たちも、日本の事情を知りたがります。これだけあればもう困らない。日米冠婚葬祭マニュアル、バイリンガル版。

まんが 日本昔ばなし
Once Upon a Time in Japan

川内彩友美 [編]　　ラルフ・マッカーシー [訳]　　160ページ　ISBN 4-7700-2173-9

人気TVシリーズ「まんが日本昔ばなし」から、「桃太郎」、「金太郎」、「一寸法師」など、より抜きの名作8話をラルフ・マッカーシーの名訳でお届けします。ホームステイなどでも役に立つ一冊です。

ベスト・オブ 宮沢賢治短編集
The Tales of Miyazawa Kenji

宮沢賢治 [著]　　ジョン・ベスター [訳]　　208ページ　ISBN 4-7700-2081-3

「注文の多い料理店」「どんぐりと山猫」「祭の晩」「鹿踊りのはじまり」「土神ときつね」「オツベルと象」「毒もみの好きな署長さん」「セロ弾きのゴーシュ」の代表作8編を精選。ジョン・ベスターの名訳でどうぞ。

銀河鉄道の夜
Night Train to the Stars

宮沢賢治 [著]　　ジョン・ベスター [訳]　　176ページ　ISBN 4-7700-2131-3

賢治童話の中でも最も人気の高い「銀河鉄道の夜」は、賢治の宗教心と科学精神が反映された独特の世界──天空、自然、大地がみごとに描かれ、光と音と動きに満ち溢れています。ジョバンニと一緒に銀河を旅してみませんか。

ベスト・オブ 窓ぎわのトットちゃん
Best of Totto-chan: The Little Girl at the Window

黒柳徹子 [著]　　ドロシー・ブリトン [訳]　　232ページ　ISBN 4-7700-2127-5

小学校一年生にして"退学"になったトットちゃんは、転校先の校長先生に「君は本当はいい子なんだよ」と温かい言葉のシャワーで励まされます……バイリンガル版で、あの空前の大ベストセラーの感動をもう一度！

マザー・グース　愛される唄70選
Mother Goose: 70 Nursery Rhymes

谷川俊太郎 [訳]　　渡辺 茂 [解説]　　176ページ　ISBN 4-7700-2078-3

「マイ・フェア・レディー」や「お熱いのがお好き」という題名も、マザー・グースからの引用だったってこと、ご存じでしたか？　英米人にとって必須教養であるこの童謡集を、詩人・谷川俊太郎の名訳と共にお楽しみください。

対訳：英語で話す日本経済Q＆A
A Bilingual Guide to the Japanese Economy

NHK国際経済プロジェクト・
大和総研経済調査部［編］

46判 (128 x 188 mm)　仮製　360ページ
ISBN 4-7700-1942-4

NHK国際放送で好評を得た番組が本になりました。
クイズと会話形式で楽しく読んでいくうちに、日本
経済の仕組が分かり、同時に英語にも強くなってい
きます。日本語と英語の対応がひと目で分かる編集
上の工夫もいっぱい。

インスタントビジネス日英会話
すぐに役立つコミュニケーションの秘訣
Instant Business Japanese
Real-Life Skills for Real-Life Situations

ジャイルズ・マリー［著］

46判 (128 x 188 mm)　仮製　272ページ
ISBN 4-7700-2105-4

面白く、簡単に読める会話形式で、いざというとき、
すぐに役立つビジネスコミュニケーションの例文200
を収録しました。キーワードは日本語と英語が対照
できるように太字で表示されています。欧米のビジ
ネスマインドと言葉を解説する「物知り英語ノート」
付き。

バイリンガル とってもかんたんマイレシピ
Stone Soup—Easy Japanese Home Cooking

渡辺節子［著］

B5判変型 (189 x 257 mm) 仮製 256ページ
ISBN 4-7700-2061-9

手軽な日本の家庭料理、わが家の味160品目の作り方を英語と日本語で紹介したクッキングブック。作り方や調理器具などのイラスト付き、カロリー計算、調理時間もひと目で分かります。

対訳：おくのほそ道
The Narrow Road to Oku

松尾芭蕉［著］　ドナルド・キーン［訳］
宮田雅之［切り絵］

A5判変型 (140 x 226 mm)
仮製 188ページ （カラー口絵41ページ）
ISBN 4-7700-2028-7

古典文学の最高峰のひとつ、「おくのほそ道」をドナルド・キーンが新訳しました。画家、宮田雅之が精魂を込めた41点のカラー切り絵の魅力とあいまって、この名作に新しい生命が吹き込まれた、必読の1冊です。

英文版 ジャパン：四季と文化
Japan: The Cycle of Life

［序文］高円宮憲仁親王殿下
［イントロダクション］C.W. ニコル

A4判変型 (228 x 297 mm)
上製 296ページ （オールカラー）
ISBN 4-7700-2088-0

日本の文化は「四季」によって育まれてきました。日本人の生活、文化、精神から切り離せないこの「四季」を、美しく新鮮な数々のカラー写真でビジュアルに紹介します。

第1部　自然と風土
第2部　人々の暮らしと伝統行事
第3部　文化と伝統

英語と日本語で楽しむ

対訳 サザエさん 全12巻
The Wonderful World of Sazae-san

長谷川町子［著］

- 吹き出しの中にオリジナルの暖かい雰囲気を大切にした英語、コマの横に日本語が付く対訳形式。

- お正月、こいのぼり、忘年会など日本独特の文化や習慣には、欄外に英語の解説つき。

46判変型　**(113 x 188 mm)**　仮製

第1巻	170ページ	ISBN 4-7700-2075-9
第2巻	168ページ	ISBN 4-7700-2093-7
第3巻	198ページ	ISBN 4-7700-2094-5
第4巻	164ページ	ISBN 4-7700-2149-6
第5巻	176ページ	ISBN 4-7700-2150-X
第9巻	172ページ	ISBN 4-7700-2154-2
第10巻	172ページ	ISBN 4-7700-2155-0
第11巻	176ページ	ISBN 4-7700-2156-9
第12巻	168ページ	ISBN 4-7700-2157-7

刊行予定

97年12月	第6巻
98年1月	第7巻、第8巻